BATHROOM BOOK
of
BRITISH COLUMBIA TRIVIA

Weird, Wacky and Wild

Andrew Fleming

BLUE BIKE BOOKS

The Publisher: Blue Bike Books

Library and Archives Canada Cataloguing in Publication

Fleming, Andrew, 1972–
　Bathroom book of British Columbia trivia: weird, wacky and wild /
Andrew Fleming.

　(Bathroom books of Canada ; 5)
　ISBN-13: 978-1-897278-02-4
　ISBN-10: 1-897278-02-0

　1. British Columbia—Miscellanea.　I. Title.　II. Series.

　FC3811.F64 2006　　　　971.1　　　　C2006-902989-X

Project Director: Nicholle Carrière
Project Editor: Audrey McClellan
Cover Image: Roger Garcia
Illustrations: Roger Garcia

PC: P5

DEDICATION

To Peter and Diane, for all their support and for instilling a love of books.

ACKNOWLEDGMENTS

Gratitude galore to my publisher for giving me this opportunity and to eagle-eyed editor extraordinaire Audrey McClellan for her invaluable assistance.

CONTENTS

INTRODUCTION

Canadians generally don't like to brag, and this cliché characteristic is reflected in the often-cryptic slogans we slap on our licence plates. Ontario, for example, merely suggests it is "Yours To Discover," while Québec, with *Je me souviens*, makes mention of remembering something it fails to specify. Saskatchewan mysteriously lays claim to being the "Land of Living Skies," Alberta acknowledges it has plenty of wild roses, PEI points out that seatbelts save lives, New Brunswick reminds people it is also *Nouveau* Brunswick, and so on. The country's westernmost province, however, deviates from the national norm by boldly boasting of being "Beautiful British Columbia."

But then, false modesty aside, there really is no better word to describe the place. Ask anyone who's ever been here. From its snowcapped mountain ranges and towering ancient rainforests to distinctive Haida art and totem poles, ocean sunsets and Pamela Anderson swimsuit calendars, there is no disputing British Columbia is easy on the eyes. While it is justly famous around the world for its natural beauty, though, many people don't seem to know much else about the province or its history.

To make a long story short, then: the first First Nations people arrived here some 15,000 years ago after trekking over the Bering Strait from Asia. Europeans dropped by uninvited in the mid-18th century when the intrepid Captain Cook was searching in vain for the Northwest Passage. Although he didn't find a watery shortcut back to England, he did find plenty of animals to skin to help feed Europe's insatiable appetite for furry hats. The Union Jack was soon planted on "Vancouver's Island," and Victoria was established as a remote outpost for the Hudson's Bay Company. When gold was discovered on the Fraser River in 1857, the Brits decided to claim the mainland, then known as New Caledonia, for themselves as well in order to keep it out of

American clutches. This turned out to have been a good move when an even bigger strike was found in the northern interior in 1862. Five years later they merged the two colonies and called it British Columbia. And in 1871, after being bribed with the promise of a railway that would link it with the other British North American colonies, the province became part of Canada.

A rather more informative and detailed account of all this can be found in *The Bathroom Book of British Columbia History*. This particular restroom reader, however, is more concerned with flushing out little-known facts and such nuggets of local esoterica as:

☛ How the NHL tradition of waving white towels was born...

☛ What musical group once featured both Jimi Hendrix and Tommy Chong as members...

☛ Where to find a polka-dotted lake or a restaurant made entirely of logging cable...

☛ Who first coined the terms *hardcore, cyberspace* and *McJob*...

☛ Where to find the world's largest cuckoo clock, fishing rod or toy soldier...

☛ Who was the first person to land a quadruple back flip on skis...

☛ How First Nations explain the reason spirit bears are white...

☛ Who was the very first comic-book superhero or paid TV performer...

☛ Why Michael J. Fox chose his middle initial...

☛ What literary masterpiece was written in a squatter's shack...

☛ What else the letters BC are an abbreviation for...

BC isn't just beautiful, it's also beguiling and a land chock full of contradictions. It is known as the Wet Coast for its prodigious precipitation, yet parts of the province receive more annual sunshine than Florida. Other people call it the Left Coast for its supposedly liberal politics, yet the current service-slashing Liberal government is about as right wing as they come. It is a place where at least half a dozen languages are more commonly heard on the streets than Canada's "other" official tongue, and a place that inexplicably chose an inukshuk, a symbol of the distant Arctic, as the logo for the 2010 Winter Olympics. There's a part of Vancouver called Gastown without any gas stations; the economy's largest cash crop is an illegal drug; and a fixer-upper one-bedroom home might sell for half a million bucks.

Lotusland, Lalaland, *Colombie-Britannique* or Canada's answer to California—whatever one calls BC, most residents will agree it is the best part of the best country in the world.

EARLY EXPLORATION

First Contact

While most history books credit the famous English explorer Captain James Cook as the first European to set foot on British Columbia in 1778, his countryman Sir Francis Drake may have beat him to it by a good 200 years. New evidence has emerged suggesting Drake, the first person to successfully circumnavigate the globe, made it as far north as the Queen Charlotte Islands in 1579. But the maps Drake drew were purposely misleading because he believed he'd found the fabled Northwest Passage, and he didn't want the Spanish, who were also exploring the Pacific at the time, to find out about it. His crew was sworn to secrecy about the voyage under penalty of death.

Far East Meets West

Some people believe a Chinese Muslim eunuch first explored the BC coast as early as 1412. Recent "evidence" to support the claim that Admiral Zheng sailed a great fleet of junks around the globe, discovering BC en route, is an 18th-century copy of a map dated 1418. According to the map's owner, Chinese businessman Liu Gang, he purchased it for $500 USD from a Shanghai dealer in 2001. The map shows accurate depictions of the North and South American coastline, although it also shows details of the two continents' interiors that no sailor could possibly have known, which makes its authenticity doubtful. There is nothing concrete to indicate it wasn't simply copied from an 18th-century European map instead of an ancient Chinese one.

The Chinese Connection

In 1882, some miners working a streambank near Telegraph Creek stumbled upon a string of 3000-year-old bronze Chinese coins. When they were hauled up from their resting place several feet below the surface, the wire holding them together disintegrated. While it is possible that Chinese miners who were in the area a few years earlier may have left the coins to stake their claim to the land, several years later a Chinese court interpreter from Victoria met Natives who showed him several ancient Buddhist silver ceremonial dishes and a number of brass charms. The sources of these items remain a mystery.

STUFF ABOUT BC

Birthdate

British Columbia celebrates its birthday on the first Monday of August, although this is more for convenience than historical accuracy. While Vancouver Island was first declared a Crown colony on January 13, 1849, and mainland British Columbia became a colony on August 2, 1858, the two were officially joined in a shotgun wedding on August 6, 1866. Since nobody particularly wants a day off work in January, and every other province was already getting a much-needed summer long weekend on that particular Monday, it was decided this was close enough to the actual date. A Leo, British Columbia shares its birthday with the likes of Bolivia, poet Alfred Lord Tennyson, scientist Sir Alexander Fleming, comedian Lucille Ball, artist Andy Warhol, Jamaica, and pop tart Gerri "Ginger Spice" Halliwell. British Columbia joined Confederation on July 20, 1871.

Namesake

While the colony of Vancouver's Island (the possessive was later dropped) was named for and by explorer George Vancouver in the 1790s, most of the mainland region was originally known as New Caledonia because of its resemblance to the Scottish Highlands (at least in the northeast corner). However, since that name was already being used in the South Pacific, Queen Victoria chose to call the new colony "Columbia," a name that had been applied to the whole region when the Hudson's Bay Company's empire included the British Columbia mainland, Washington, Idaho and Oregon. To differentiate it from other Columbias in existence, she emphasized that it was "British Columbia."

Population

There were an estimated 4,220,000 British Columbians in 2005. Urbanites make up roughly 85 percent of the population, while the remaining 15 percent live in rural areas.

Official Signs and Symbols

Flower: The Pacific dogwood (*Cornus nuttallii*) has been considered an unofficial emblem since 1931, when the Dogwood Protection Act was passed to prohibit cutting or picking its flowers on public land. It was officially adopted in 1956. The dogwood grows six to eight metres high, flowers in the springtime and sports bunches of bright red berries in the fall.

Bird: The Steller's jay (*Cyanocitta stelleri*), which is considered a pest by farmers, was chosen as British Columbis's avian emblem after a province-wide mail-in vote in 1987. It narrowly defeated the more majestic peregrine falcon. The trumpeter swan came in a distant third.

Gemstone: BC jade is known as an extremely tough material and was initially used by First Nations for knives and axe heads. The green gem later became prized by carvers of fine jewellery and sculptures and was named the official mineral in 1968. BC is home to half the jade in the world.

Tree: First Nations used western red cedar (*Thuja plicata*) for just about everything: homes, canoes, totem poles, masks, baskets, clothing, armour, tea, boxes, tools, you name it. Even today it is one of the province's most valued resources, and it was recognized as the official tree in 1988.

Tartan: Adopted in 1974, the provincial kilt contains five colours: blue for the ocean, white for the dogwood flower, green for the forests, red for the maple leaf, and gold for the crown and the sun on the provincial shield and flag.

ON THE GROUND

Size Matters

There are only 30 countries in the world larger than Canada's third-largest province. With an area of nearly one million square kilometres, BC is four times the size of the UK and two and a half times the size of Japan. It is approximately 1450 kilometres from top to bottom.

Top of the Province

Located along the Alaska border, the 4663-metre summit of Mount Fairweather is the highest point in BC and the 10th highest in Canada. Captain James Cook gave the mountain its name in 1778 after spotting the peak during a brief period of clear skies while exploring the coast. But the weather around Mount Fairweather is usually anything but fair. Located not far inland from the ocean, the region is subjected to storms year-round and has average temperatures of –45°C. A team of Canadians (Allen Carpé, William Ladd, Andy Taylor and Terris Moore) first reached the summit in 1931.

The highest point located entirely within provincial borders is 4019-metre-high Mount Waddington, near the head of Bute Inlet in the southwestern Pacific Range of the Coast Mountains. The local Coast Salish believed the mountain was the keeper of the inlet's notorious winds. It remained uncharted until first sighted by mountaineers Don and Phyllis Munday while they were on a climbing trip on Vancouver Island in 1925. They named the distinctive peak, which is often compared to Europe's famous Mont Blanc massif, "Mystery Mountain," but were overruled by the Geographic Board of Canada. The new name honoured Alfred Waddington, whose failed dream was to build a road from Bute Inlet to the Interior. Mount Waddington was first climbed by Americans Fritz Wiessner and William House in 1936.

Pacific Heights

The tallest underwater mountain located within Canadian waters is known as the Bowies Seamount. Approximately 3000 metres high, it is located about 200 kilometres west of the Queen Charlotte Islands and about 20 metres below the surface of the ocean.

The Centre of Things

The geographical centre of BC is marked by a cairn in the town of Weneez, just east of Vanderhoof. *Weneez* is a Dakelh First Nation word meaning, appropriately enough, "centre."

Legendary Falls

Della Falls is the highest waterfall in Canada and 10th highest in the world. Located in Strathcona Provincial Park on Vancouver Island, the falls are the result of Drinkwater Creek falling 440 metres into Della Lake. To see Della, take a boat across Great Central Lake (near Port Alberni) to the trailhead. From there it is about a day's hike to the base of the falls.

DID YOU KNOW?

Four more of Canada's six highest waterfalls, all of which dwarf Niagara Falls even if they don't see as many tourists, are found in British Columbia. In descending order, they are:

- Takakkaw Falls (Yoho National Park)—254 metres
- Hunlen Falls (Tweedsmuir Park)—253 metres
- Helmcken Falls (Wells Gray Park)—137 metres
- Bridal Veil Falls (Bridal Veil Provincial Park)—122 metres

The strongest currents in the world are known as the Nakwakto Rapids. Located in Slingsby Channel, just north of Port Hardy, their flow rate can reach 16 knots or (for landlubbers) nearly 30 kilometres per hour.

ROLLING ON THE RIVER

Mythic River

Its headwaters rise in the Rocky Mountains near Jasper National Park, and it eventually drains into the ocean at Vancouver, which makes the 1399-kilometre-long Fraser River the province's longest waterway and the fifth longest in Canada. The first white guy to stumble upon it was explorer Alexander Mackenzie, who in 1793 was searching for a route to the Pacific. Local natives advised him to go overland rather than attempt to descend via the river; advice he wisely followed. The first white man to travel down the river was North West Company fur-trading trailblazer Simon Fraser, who (under the misimpression it was actually the strategically vital Columbia River) led a 35-day expedition from present-day Fort Saint James to the river's mouth in 1808.

Knocking on Hell's Door

Fraser embarked with four canoes, 21 employees and two Native guides. They were lucky to escape with their lives from the treacherous white water of the Fraser Canyon—particularly the narrow stretch known today as Hell's Gate, where the river is funnelled through a gorge only 30 metres wide. They managed to portage that section, and the route was abandoned as a potential fur-trading route.

Simon Fraser Says

"I cannot find words to describe our situation at times. We had to pass where no human beings should venture."

Dubious Honour

Fellow explorer and mapmaker David Thompson, who successfully navigated the elusive Columbia in 1811, later named the river "Fraser" in his peer's honour. Fraser's sentiments about this were not recorded.

The River File

Ten of Canada's dozen longest rivers run through British Columbia. After the Fraser, they are:

- Columbia River: 763 km
- Skeena River: 621 km
- Stikine River: 589 km
- Thompson River: 534 km
- Nechako River: 516 km
- Kootenay River: 508 km
- Nass River: 380 km
- Finlay River: 306 km
- Fort Nelson River: 305 km

(Length given is within BC.)

GREAT LAKES

Lippy Lake

Babine Lake is BC's largest (497 km²) and longest (177 kilometres) natural lake found entirely within provincial borders. Located 36 kilometres north of the town of Burns Lake, it is part of the traditional territory of the Nat'oot'en people of the Dakelh First Nation. *Babine* is a French word meaning "large lip," a reference to the local custom of wearing jewellery in the lower lip. The Nat'oot'en call the lake Na-taw-bun-kut, meaning, appropriately enough, "long lake."

Warm Waters

With midsummer temperatures averaging around 24°C, Christina Lake in Gladstone Provincial Park near Grand Forks is considered Canada's warmest lake. Kimberly residents make the same claim for their own Wasa Lake, as do Osoyoosians of Osoyoos Lake. All are popular places to hang out on a summer's day.

Crystal Clear

The purest water in BC can be found in Tchesinkut Lake, 16 kilometres south of the town of Burns Lake. *Tchesinkut*, (pronounced te-sing-kut) is a Dakelh word meaning "clear waters," and the lake is a popular sport fishing destination.

Salt Lake Pretty

Travellers heading west from the border town of Osoyoos often do a double take when they see a polka-dotted lake just off the highway. The dots, which look like giant lily pads, are actually salt pans and are most noticeable in summers with little rain. The 12-hectare privately owned Spotted Lake has heavy concentrations of various dissolved minerals, including copper, silver, gold, sulphates and Epsom salts, that rise to the surface to form plates that dot the lake's surface. Natives called the lake Kliluk, or "medicine lake," and believed that a soak in its waters brought both youth and wisdom. According to one legend, warring tribes once called a time out so that both sides could bathe their wounded there.

WOODS AND DESERTS

In the Woods

BC is home to about a quarter of the world's remaining temperate rainforests. While they once blanketed the mainland's coastal shores and much of Vancouver Island, only a few areas have never been logged. The Kitlope Valley, which lies between Bella Coola and Kitimat on the northwest coast, is the world's largest untouched ancient rainforest.

Top Trees

Canada's tallest tree is a 95-metre-high Sitka spruce that stands hidden somewhere in Carmanah Walbran Provincial Park on Vancouver Island. Although estimated to be only around 400 years old, it towers above its surrounding 1000-year-old elder relatives.

DID YOU KNOW?

The tallest example of BC's official tree, the red cedar, stands 60 metres high with a base 6 metres around and can be found at Cheewaht Lake in Pacific Rim National Park.

Robust Desert

While the BC Interior is known for being hot and dry, only a tiny part of it actually qualifies as a desert. The Okanagan Pocket Desert is a continuation of the Sonoran Desert, and the plants and animals found there are the same as those that inhabit the higher elevations of the Mexican portion of this desert. It is one of Canada's most endangered ecosystems and home to sage, prickly pear cactus and several species of rare animals; 22 percent of BC's endangered birds, mammals, reptiles and amphibians live there.

WHITHER THE WEATHER

They say if you don't like the weather in BC, wait five minutes and it'll probably change. The Wet Coast is the proud holder of the most weather-related records in Canada.

Hot Stuff

There is a heated rivalry between the Interior towns of Lytton and Lillooet over which is the hottest place in Canada. Both lay claim to a record high of 44.4°C on July 16, 1941.

DID YOU  KNOW?

Lytton was named after Edward Bulwer-Lytton, who penned the immortal line: "It was a dark and stormy night..."

It's Not the Heat...It's the Humidity

Nearby Kamloops also lays claim to being the hottest city in Canada after enduring 24 straight days of temperatures over 35°C in 1958.

Soaking Up the Sun

Cranbrook, the largest city in the Rocky Mountain region, lays claim to being BC's sunniest spot and receives around 2250 hours of prime UV rays each year. Victoria, however, holds the record for the longest sunny stretch: 2426 hours in 1970 (interrupted only by nightfall). The garden city also hosted Canada's longest frost-free period over 685 balmy days in 1925 and 1926. All of Canada's apricots, 60 percent of its cherries, half its pears and prunes, 30 percent of its apples and 20 percent of its peaches are grown in BC's sunny Okanagan Valley, which receives more sunshine annually than Florida.

Ahead in the Clouds

Prince Rupert is considered Canada's least sunny city, with an average of 6123 hours of overcast skies each year.

Wet Coast

The rainiest day in Canadian history occurred in Ucluelet, on Vancouver Island's west coast, on October 6, 1967, when 1870 millimetres fell from the sky. The longest continuous downpour was recorded in the Queen Charlotte Islands, where it rained for 300 days and 300 nights in 1939. About 25 billion litres of water falls from the sky each day in BC.

Uncommon Cold

The coldest day in the Great White North's recorded history took place at Smith River in the northwest corner of BC. The mercury dropped to –59°C one long January night in 1947.

Let It Snow

BC holds all Canadian snowfall records. Mount Fidelity in Glacier National Park sees the most snow on any given year, with around 1435 centimetres. The most snow in one season, 2447 centimetres, piled up on top of Mount Copeland, near Revelstoke, in 1972. The most in a month was 536 centimetres, burying Highway 3 in the St. Elias Range in 1959, and the most in a day was 145 centimetres at Tahtsa Lake in 1999.

DISASTER AREAS

Avalanche!

Canada's deadliest avalanche occurred on March 5, 1910, at Roger's Pass, where the Canadian Pacific Railway once wound through the treacherous Selkirk Mountains. After a slide from one side of the valley covered a section of the track, the 62 workers who were clearing it were hit by another avalanche from the other side and were buried under 10 metres of snow. This was but the worst example of the many fatal slides that occurred between 1885 and 1911—200 railway workers were killed on the job during this period, and the CPR eventually decided to abandon the route and build tunnels through the mountains instead.

1915   Fifty-seven people died in a slide at Britannia Beach near Vancouver.

1965   Twenty-six miners died at the Granduc Mining Camp near the Alaska border.

1979   Seven heli-skiers were killed in the Purcell Range near Golden.

1981   Three heli-skiers were killed on the Conrad Icefield, also near Golden.

1987   Seven heli-skiers died in the Cariboo Range near Blue River.

1991   Nine heli-skiers died in Bugaboo Glacier Provincial Park.

1998   Michel Trudeau, youngest son of the former prime minister Pierre Elliott Trudeau, was killed on a backcountry ski trip when he was swept into Lake Kokanee. His body has never been recovered.

2003   Seven heli-skiers, including legendary snowboarder Craig Kelly, died on the Durrand Glacier in the Selkirk Mountains near Revelstoke. Later the same year, seven students from Calgary's Strathcona-Tweedsmuir School were killed while on a backcountry ski trip near Golden.

A Mighty Wind

Typhoon Freda hit the southwest corner of BC on October 12, 1962, with winds recorded at up to 145 kilometres per hour. Seven people were killed and nearly a quarter of Vancouver's Stanley Park was flattened.

On Shaky Ground

Sooner or later the province is going to be hit with a major earthquake. Just west of Vancouver Island, the Juan de Fuca tectonic plate, which had been sliding under the North American plate, has become stuck, and the pressure to continue moving keeps on building. Something's got to give, and when it does, experts predict the quake will last several minutes and leave coastal regions up to 2 metres lower than they are now.

Shaking All Over

The largest earthquake in Canadian history, with a magnitude of 8.1 on the Richter Scale, occurred off the Queen Charlotte Islands on August 22, 1949. The shaking was so intense that it knocked people and even cows off their feet.

Surf's Up

On March 27, 1964, another major quake took place off the coast of Alaska, creating a tsunami that killed 100 people in this remote corner of the world. The wave then swept south towards British Columbia at a speed of 720 kilometres per hour. In Port Alberni on Vancouver Island's west coast, waves swept through town, uprooting trees, destroying homes and carrying away cars. Amazingly, nobody was killed. Damage was estimated at $10 million.

Rocking the Rockies

The largest Canadian on-land quake had a magnitude of 7.3 and took place under central Vancouver Island on June 23, 1946. Felt as far away as Alberta, the quake knocked down 75 percent of the chimneys in nearby Courtenay and Cumberland. One person drowned as a result of the quake, and another died from a heart attack.

Vulcan Greeting

Chances are that a major quake would also wake up a dormant volcano or two. While all has been quiet on the western volcanic front for many years now, about 2000 years ago, Meager Mountain, located in the Garibaldi Volcanic Belt north of Vancouver, erupted with the force of 10 hydrogen bombs.

Tierra Del Fuego

There is only one volcano known to have taken human life in what is now Canada, and its eruption just happened to coincide with the arrival of the first European explorers in 1775. Among the first things that Juan Francisco de la Bodega y Quadra and his crew aboard the *Sonora* saw when they dropped anchor was an eruption. The Spanish crew described "great flames which issued from four or five mouths of a volcano and at nighttime lit up the whole district, rendering everything visible."

In the Line of Fire

From their safe vantage at sea, the new arrivals had no idea that on land an estimated 2000 members of two Nisga'a tribes perished in the eruption. In 1935, anthropologist Marius Barbeau journeyed up the Nass River and spoke with many elders who told vivid stories of the eruption and its aftermath. According to the Nisga'a, the eruption was a consequence of some youngsters angering the Salmon Spirit by disrespecting a humpback salmon caught in the Nass River.

BC BEASTS

Blue Bird of Lotusland

In 1987, students across British Columbia chose the Steller's jay to be the official provincial bird. Often mistaken for a blue jay, it is a member of the Corvidae family, considered to be one of the most intelligent and adaptable family of birds in the world. It was named after Georg Steller, a German naturalist who accompanied Vitus Bering on his trip when he discovered the Bering Strait in 1728.

DID YOU  KNOW?

Despite the Steller jay's status as BC's official bird, farmers consider them to be nothing more than pests that endanger crops and profits.

Animals of the State

In 1895, King Edward VII chose two lucky beasts to appear on BC's coat of arms. They are a wapiti stag and a bighorn sheep. The wapiti (or deer) of Vancouver Island and the bighorn sheep of the mountainous mainland symbolize the two colonies that united to form the province.

Faster Pussycat

Vancouver Island is home to the greatest concentration of mountain lions, or cougars, in North America. The largest puma in Canada, cougars run at an average speed of 35 kilometres per hour, can spring over 5 metres and are capable of killing an animal six times their own weight. Fortunately, they prefer to eat species other than us, though attacks on humans are on the rise as cougar habitats continue to shrink. There have been 110 documented attacks (16 fatal) in North America since 1890, yet almost half of them happened after 1990. Good thing the island has plenty of wapiti to go around.

DID YOU  KNOW?

If you ever find yourself facing a hungry cougar, try to make yourself seem as large as possible. And fight back if attacked—the best place to hit them is in the nose. Climbing trees or playing dead are definite *no-nos*.

One of a Kind Bear

Don't call them polar bears. The Kermode, or spirit, bear is a genetic offshoot of the black bear that is whiter than the average polar bear. They range along the north and central coast and many are found in the recently protected Great Bear Rainforest, one of the world's last unspoiled temperate rainforests, which stretches 400 kilometres and covers two million hectares.

Legends about the spirit bear date its origin to the end of the ice age. Local folklore has it that when the glaciers retreated, Raven, the creator, flew over the area, making the land lush and green, but turned every 10th bear white to act as a reminder of a time when ice and snow covered the world.

DID YOU  KNOW?

Baby bears are usually born in winter. The cubs, born blind and defenceless, stay in the den until spring, when the mother wakes and finally takes them out for some food.

Black & White & Spread All Over

Few creatures are as closely associated with British Columbia as the orca. Although they are the most widely distributed mammal on Earth after humans, their population is concentrated in the waters of the Pacific Northwest, and they figure prominently in the religion and artwork of the local First Nations.

Although they are also known as "killer whales," this is a misnomer as orcas are neither. They are actually a species of dolphin, not a whale, and there's never been an attack (let alone a fatal one) on a human by an orca in the wild. They have, however, occasionally been known to attack their captors at marine theme parks.

Killer Killers

The only known killer killer whales in history were three orcas at Victoria's Sealand, who drowned 20-year-old trainer Keltie Byrne after she fell into their tank in 1991. Many believe they were only trying to play and didn't know she, unlike them, couldn't last long underwater.

Camel Tow

During BC's gold rush of 1862, someone had the bright idea of importing camels to hump supplies up the Cariboo Wagon Road alongside the Fraser River to the goldfields. It probably seemed like a good idea at the time, but the beasts were more used to soft desert sand, so special booties had to be made to protect their feet from the rocky road. They also bit and kicked at other animals and people, and after four months they were banned from travelling on the road. Some managed to escape into the wild but never adapted to the BC environment and were eventually wiped out.

Octopus Guarded

The largest octopus in the world lives off the coast of British Columbia. The Pacific octopus can weigh up to 70 kilograms and stretch 7 metres from one of its eight arms to another. There are up to 200 suckers the size of tangerines on each arm. The giant also has the biggest and best brain of all invertebrates; researchers estimate its intelligence is on a par with a housecat.

Batland

British Columbia is the battiest place in Canada. Most of the 16 bat species living in the province can be found in the warm Okanagan region. Bats hate the cold and are rarely found at elevations above 1500 metres, which includes most of the province.

DID YOU  KNOW?

Members of the largest bat colony in BC, estimated at around 2000, hang out together in an abandoned church on the Little Shuswap Indian Reserve near Shuswap Lake.

Bats in the Legislature

The big brown bat, one of BC's largest flying rodents, is known to enjoy spending its winters inside the provincial legislative building in Victoria.

Chocolate Snack

As you might guess from its name, the Vancouver Island marmot is only found on Vancouver Island. Considered one of the world's rarest mammals and Canada's most endangered species, the VI marmot is distinguished from its common cousin, the hoary marmot, by its chocolate brown fur. A recovery program hopes to increase the marmot's numbers through captive breeding. Hope it works, as there were fewer than 40 in the wild at the end of 2005, and they remain the preferred snack for the Island's many wolves, cougars, hawks and black bears.

ROADSIDE ATTRACTIONS

A few of British Columbia's biggest things.

WORLD'S HEAVIEST HOCKEY STICK

Hockey is big everywhere in Canada, but nowhere more so than in the Vancouver Island community of Duncan, home to a 63-metre-long hockey stick weighing nearly three tonnes. Made of Douglas fir and reinforced with steel, the giant lumber (roughly 40 times the size of a normal stick) was built for display at Expo 86 in Vancouver and was shipped to Duncan after the city won a Canada-wide competition to be home ice.

WORLD'S TALLEST TOTEM POLE

Known as the Spirit of Lekwammen ("Land of the Winds"), this 55-metre-tall totem pole, carved from a single ancient red cedar, was raised as part of the opening ceremonies of the 1994 Commonwealth Games held in Victoria. Alas, safety concerns were soon also raised, and fears that an airplane might eventually crash into it led to the pole being downsized to a 12-metre-high mere shadow of its former self. Only slightly shorter than the original Spirit of Lekwammen, at 53-metres, the tallest totem still standing can be found in Alert Bay at the northern end of Vancouver Island. Made of two trees rather than just one, it was carved by six Kwakwaka'wakw artists to represent various tribes of their nation.

WORLD'S LARGEST CUCKOO CLOCK

Every hour on the hour in the Rocky Mountain town of
Kimberley, "Happy Hans" emerges from a titanic timepiece
to yodel the new time. The life-size, lederhosened figure is but
one of many Bavarian quirks adopted to mark the town's status
as one of Canada's highest cities (1113 metres above sea level).
Accordion music wheezes merrily from the town square (also
known as the "Platzl"), while gingerbread trim and brightly
coloured shutters adorn the town's houses.

WORLD'S LONGEST PAIR OF SKIS

Thought your skis were expensive? 100 Mile House, the self-proclaimed "International Nordic Ski Capital," is home to a pair of 12-metre-long Karhu cross-country racing skis with 9-metre poles. The giant skinny skis can be found at the former gold rush town's visitor information centre and were planted there to draw attention to the region's vast network of groomed ski trails.

WORLD'S HEFTIEST FISHING ROD

Warner Jarvis had a dream. Hoping that if he built it, they would come ("they" being tourists), he spearheaded a project in the rural northern town of Houston to construct a giant fly-fishing rod to bolster the town's claim to be the "Steelhead Capital of the World." Nearly 20 metres long and weighing 360 kilograms, the aluminum rod was built with time and materials donated by 40 different local businesses.

WORLD'S GRANDEST GOLD PAN

The historic gold-rush boomtown of Quesnel bills itself the "Gold Pan City," so it should come as no surprise that it features an enormous gold pan 5.5 metres tall and weighing nearly 1400 kilograms. The tiny Yukon community of Burwash Landing, however, stakes the same claim with a giant pan of its own.

WORLD'S LARGEST TREE CRUSHER

The rural northern BC community of Mackenzie is home to a 175-tonne machine used in the 1960s to clear timber from the Rocky Mountain Trench during the building of the W.A.C. Bennett Dam. The town now lies on Williston Lake, the largest human-made reservoir in North America, which was created after the dam backed up the Peace River for over 200 kilometres.

WORLD'S TALLEST TIN SOLDIER

This 10-metre-tall statue on the bank of the Fraser River in New Westminster is actually made of stainless steel. It was built to commemorate the soldiers of the Royal Engineers, who built the embryonic town's first structures back in 1864. Located next to the public market, the tin man contains a time capsule (but no heart), to be opened in 2025.

World's Biggest Burl

Burls, the knotty warts that develop when extra cells grow on a tree, are usually used for making things such as tabletops or clocks. Unless, like the one carved from a giant Sitka spruce near Holberg on northern Vancouver Island in 2005, they are too big for anything but being put on display. The burl, which is 6 metres tall, 6 metres wide and weighs an estimated 30 tonnes, can be found at a waterfront park in downtown Port McNeill.

World's Most Monstrous Truck

After eight separate railway cars delivered it in pieces in 1978, the giant Terex Titan was assembled in the Rocky Mountain town of Sparwood to work in the local coalmines. Twenty metres long, 8 metres wide and 7 metres tall, the monster truck's maximum load is 350 tonnes, and its box is big enough to hold two Greyhound buses. Currently on display outside the Sparwood Chamber of Commerce along Highway 3, it was retired in 1990 after becoming too expensive to operate.

World's Longest Suspension Bridge

Located 70 metres above the Capilano River in North Vancouver, the wobbly Capilano Suspension Bridge is the Lower Mainland's oldest attraction and its second most popular after the Vancouver Aquarium. The 137-metre-long bridge was first built with hemp rope and cedar planks by Scottish civil engineer George Grant Mackay in 1888. Natives called it the "laughing bridge" because of the noise it made when wind blew through the canyon. After Mackay's death, the sketchy structure was replaced by a wire cable bridge in 1903. Around 750,000 people inch their way across the bridge each year. In the past, visitors have included celebrities such as Mick Jagger, Marilyn Monroe and Margaret Thatcher.

DID YOU KNOW?

On September 22, 1999, Nadia Hama somehow dropped her disabled 18-month-old daughter, Kaya, off the bridge. Miraculously, the baby survived the fall unscathed after branches helped break her fall. Police recommended charging Hama with attempted murder, but no charges were laid because of lack of evidence. Hama later sued the bridge's owners for not sufficiently warning her to be careful when crossing the precarious swinging structure while carrying a baby. The case was settled out of court.

RECORD BREAKERS

WORLD'S MOST GIGANTIC GINGERBREAD MAN

Chefs at Vancouver's Hyatt Regency Hotel baked the monster cookie on November 19, 2003. The gingerbread giant measured over four metres in height and weighed a whopping 169 kilograms. Its ingredients included 100 kilos of flour, 20 kilos of shortening, 20 kilos of sugar and 20 kilos of molasses.

WORLD'S LENGTHIEST TELEGRAM

Reportedly nearly a kilometre long, the telegram was a petition signed by 177,000 Canadians and sent to the White House in 1969 to protest nuclear testing on the Aleutian island of Amchitka. It took Western Union four days to deliver the message.

WORLD'S WETTEST WATER FIGHT

In order to celebrate the bicentennial of Fort Nelson's incorporation in 1805, half the town's population got together one fine summer day to drench each other. Over 40,000 water balloons were tossed in less than three minutes to set a new record.

WORLD'S LARGEST EAGLE HANGOUT

Each year from November to March, thousands of bald eagles from throughout the Pacific Northwest gather along the shores of the Squamish, Cheakamus and Mamquam rivers near Brackendale to feed on the eggs and carcasses of spawned-out salmon. The largest assembly to date was in 1994, when birdwatchers counted 3766 raptors in a single day.

WORLD'S LARGEST NON-NUCLEAR PEACETIME EXPLOSION

In the late 1700s, explorer George Vancouver called the channel at Seymour Narrows in the Georgia Strait "one of the vilest stretches of water in the world." Its deadliest feature was the twin peaks of Ripple Rock, which lurked just below the surface of the water between Vancouver Island and Quadra Island. "Old Rip" was the bane of seafarers for centuries, sinking 119 vessels and taking nearly as many lives. Although the Narrows are about 120 metres deep, the south peak of Ripple Rock came within 3 metres of the surface at low tide, creating deadly waves and whirlpools as well as piercing the occasional hull. Its reign of terror came to an end on April 5, 1958, after 1375 tonnes of explosives blasted 700,000 tonnes of debris 300 metres into the air. When the dust and waves settled, the new summit of Ripple Rock lay 15 metres under the sea.

WORLD'S MOST SUBSTANTIAL SAND SCULPTURE
Measuring 6.3 metres high, "The Christmas Tree," built on
September 21, 1993, in Harrison Hot Springs, holds the record
as the tallest hand-built sculpture ever.

WORLD'S LARGEST SIMULTANEOUS BREASTFEEDING
On October 6, 2001, at 11:00 AM, 793 nursing mothers in
26 locations across the province made history by staging a mass
public breastfeeding in order to draw attention to the benefits of
mother's milk over formula.

MASSIVE MISCELLANEOUS

WORLD'S MOST EXTENSIVE AUTOMATED LIGHT TRANSIT SYSTEM

First introduced at Expo 86, Vancouver's emission-free and energy-efficient Skytrain covers 50 kilometres and 33 stations throughout the Lower Mainland. The monorail's 45-metre-long "Skybridge" over the Fraser River is the longest transit-only bridge in the world.

WORLD'S LARGEST ENVIRONMENTAL ORGANIZATION

Unhappy with American plans to detonate a weapon of mass destruction in waters off Alaska, a motley crew of activists, ecologists, journalists, hippies and draft dodgers got together to form the "Don't Make A Wave Committee" in 1971 and shipped out in an old fishing boat to try and stop the nuclear test. Since then, the group has changed its name to Greenpeace and become an international green giant that has helped make "ecology" a household word.

WORLD'S FARTHEST-SEEING TELESCOPE

Researchers at both UBC and UVic are part of a team building a 30-metre telescope that will be 100 times more powerful than the Hubble Space Telescope, with a light-collecting area nine times the size of the largest existing scope. The $750-million project is expected to be completed by 2020 and will let astronomers boldly check out things no one has checked out before.

WORLD'S LONGEST FREE FERRY

The scenic 90-minute round-trip across Kootenay Lake, the largest lake in southern BC, aboard either the MV *Balfour* or MV *Osprey* is far and away the most affordable cruise on earth. As the massive lake rarely freezes, the service is available year-round.

WORLD'S BIGGEST GRIZZLY BEAR REFUGE

The 9-hectare enclosed habitat at the Kicking Horse Ski Resort, near Golden, is home to Boo the bear, who was orphaned as a baby when some idiot shot his mother off the side of Highway 26 near Quesnel. He previously shared the space with his brother, who died in 2004. It may sound strange to have gondolas of gawkers passing overhead, but ski resorts actually make for ideal grizzly habitat because the slopes resemble avalanche paths, where all their favourite food grows. Grizzly bears are currently considered an endangered species in BC.

DID YOU KNOW?

In the spring of 2006, Boo escaped from his refuge twice, breaking down a large steel door and clearing a series of fences, and was seen cavorting with female bears in the wild. The first time he was recaptured; the second time he returned voluntarily after the four-week grizzly mating season ended. He had lost weight and his keeper thought he probably returned because there was food and safety at the refuge.

WORLD'S MOST MASSIVE MOTION CAPTURE STUDIO

The Electronic Arts building in Burnaby covers 3400 m²—including 1800 m² of studio space—and cost $11 million to build. Specializing in filming actors, athletes and stunt performers who wear special costumes with electronic markers that allow their recorded movements to be computerized, the mega-studio is a major player in the computer game market and helped create top sellers such as *NHL 2000*, *The Godfather*, *NFL Football* and *James Bond 007*.

WORLD'S HUGEST CHOPSTICK FACTORY

The reason Fort Nelson makes more chopsticks than, say, a town in China has more to do with the number of nearby aspen trees than any high local demand for the unwieldy eating utensils. Although the northern town of 5000 has only three Chinese restaurants, its Canadian Chopstick Manufacturing company pumps out seven million pairs of chopsticks a day.

WORLD'S LARGEST AIR-SUPPORTED DOMED STADIUM

Constructed in 1983 in preparation for Expo 86, BC Place is home to the BC Lions and was the first domed stadium in Canada to use air to raise its roof. Although Detroit claims its Silverdome has the biggest air-supported dome, and the Silverdome is capable of seating more people than Vancouver's 60,000-seater, BC Place has a larger playing field, and its Teflon-coated fibreglass fabric roof covers a greater area.

WORLD'S LARGEST FLOAT PLANE OPERATION

With a fleet of over 25 planes, Harbour Air is the largest all-seaplane airline. It provides regular daily service between Vancouver, Nanaimo, Victoria and the Gulf Islands as well as between Prince Rupert and the Queen Charlotte Islands.

BIG THINGS THAT GO BUMP IN BC

Tall, Dark and Ugly—In Search of Bigfoot

While Sasquatch sightings have been reported throughout North America, the bipedal being with the big feet is most closely associated with the Pacific Northwest—47 close encounters have been reported in BC alone since the first one in 1811. Witnesses generally describe a tall, hairy humanoid that reeks to high heaven. Many also report hearing distinct vocalizations—grunts and shrieks that seem very much like some sort of primitive language. While several of the sightings have been proven to be hoaxes, many people remain convinced of the mysterious creature's existence.

The word Sasquatch is taken from the Coast Salish word *sasqac*, meaning "hairy giant," and the mysterious beings figure prominently in many tribal legends throughout the province.

Planet of the Apes

Cryptozoologists suggest that, if sasquatch do exist, they are probably descendants of *Gigantopithecus*, a giant ape who lived in China five million years ago. The theory is that they would have come over on Beringia, the land bridge that once crossed the Bering Strait, along with all the other species who did so—including *Homo sapiens*. This argument is supported by the folklore of other cultures in the vicinity, in which similar creatures appear. While the Yeti (or Abominable Snowman) of the Himalayas is the best-known example, Mongolians, Afghanis, Pakistanis and the Vietnamese all tell tall tales of hairy hominids haunting their hills as well.

Real or imagined, the Sasquatch is engrained in BC culture. There is a Sasquatch Provincial Park; the "Sasquatch Daze" festival takes places annually in Harrison Hot Springs; and Kokanee, the province's top-selling beer, has been exploiting the legend in its ad campaigns for years. If you look carefully, you might see Bigfoot's likeness hidden on the labels of Kokanee bottles and cans.

DID YOU KNOW?

Bigfoot even has his very own comic-book character. Since 1979, "Sasquatch" has been a member of Marvel Comics' Canadian superhero team Alpha Flight. The story goes that after BC-born biophysics professor Walter Langkowsky exposed himself to gamma rays in an attempt to become like the Incredible Hulk, he became big, strong and hairy rather than big, strong and green.

'Pogo Shtick

"I'm looking for the Ogopogo,
His mother was a mutton,
His father was a whale,
I'm going to put a little bit of salt upon his tail."

–"The Ogopogo" by Bill Brimblecomb, 1926

Name a deep, dark lake in Canada and chances are good someone has seen something strange swimming in it. Even so, no lake monster outside of Scotland is quite as famous as Lake Okanagan's Ogopogo.

Contrary to popular belief, the palindromic moniker didn't come from a First Nations' name for the creature; to the local Okanagan Nation the monster was known as N'ha-a-itk, which translates roughly to "sacred creature of the water" or "lake demon," depending on who you ask. When crossing the lake,

Okanagan people always carried animals that could be sacrificed in the event that the creature appeared, and they never fished at Squally Point, a turbulent stretch of lake near Rattlesnake Island, where the entrance to Ogopogo's cave supposedly lies. Petroglyphs found near the headwaters of nearby Powers Creek show an ancient illustration of a serpent-like beast, and many feel this is the earliest evidence of Ogopogo's existence.

Thar She Goes

The first sightings by European settlers were in 1860, 60 years before the first recorded appearances of the Loch Ness Monster in Scotland. Most of the hundreds of people who have reported seeing Ogopogo in the years since describe a black or brown eel-like creature approximately 10 to 15 metres long. Some say it has humps on its back; others figure the humps are simply the results of snake-like swimming undulations. The largest group sighting came in 1926 when more than 30 people all reported seeing the same thing from Mission Beach. The supersized serpent was given the name Ogopogo the same year after a local man wrote a parody of a then-popular British music hall song.

DID YOU KNOW?

Mythical or not, Ogopogo is protected by provincial laws that make it illegal to capture, kill or even annoy the monster.

Other Local Loch Stalkers

Ogopogo isn't the only mysterious sea serpent said to swim the lakes of British Columbia. "Sicopogo" is the most famous resident of Shuswap Lake, while similar creatures have been reported in Osoyoos, Moberly, Harrison, Kootenay and Cultus lakes.

Who's Your Caddy?

For centuries there have been reports of a giant long-necked, horse-headed creature swimming in the sea around Vancouver Island. It has been known as Cadborosaurus (for Cadboro Bay, where the beast has most often been spotted), Caddy for short, since the *Victoria Times* held a naming contest in 1933. The Manhousat First Nation referred to it as *hiyitl'iik*—"he who moves by wriggling side to side."

There have been hundreds of reported sightings over the years, most recently in 1997, when a retired couple living in Oak Bay spotted something they described as looking like animated inner tubes bobbing outside their waterfront home. Sometimes entire groups of people have seen the creature, which is more difficult to dismiss. In February 1953, for example, at least 10 people watched for over an hour as Caddy cavorted throughout Qualicum Bay, halfway up the east coast of Vancouver Island. The following February, near Nanaimo, it is said to have put on another show for over 30 people.

See Monster?

The most compelling evidence of Caddy's existence is a photo taken long before the days of Photoshop. In July 1937, a 3.2-metre-long specimen was discovered in the stomach of a sperm whale. Photos taken at the Naden Harbour whaling station in the Queen Charlotte Islands show a snake-like creature of some sort, still fairly intact, with a horse-like head and a tail with two hind flippers. The creepy carcass was sent to Victoria for testing, but all records have since mysteriously disappeared.

DID YOU KNOW?

The Vancouver Island community of Oak Bay is offering $10,000 to anyone who can capture three-minute video footage of the local sea monster.

The Adventures of Aquaman

Long before the notable monster movie *The Creature from the Black Lagoon* came out in 1954, First Nations people were telling fishy stories about subaquatic, cannibalistic humanoids that inhabited North America's lakes, rivers and oceans. On August 19, 1972, two teenagers hanging out at Thetis Lake, a popular Victoria swimming hole, claimed to have seen a giant two-legged reptile emerge from the water. Gordon Pike and Robin Flewellyn described the silvery-scaled stranger as being around 2 metres tall, with huge pointed ears, flipper-like feet and a froggy face. It had a large, barbed fin on its head with which it lacerated one boy's hand after it gave chase. Although cops in the horror movies never seem to believe local teenagers until it is too late, Victoria RCMP were so impressed with the sincerity of the witnesses (not to mention the injured hand) that they launched a complete investigation into the attack.

The One that Got Away

Whether a hoax or not, the teens' claims were bolstered four days later when two other witnesses, who were unacquainted with the boys or their story, described seeing a similar creature near the lake. While the Mounties didn't get their man, or their man-fish, they spent several weeks scouring the lake and the surrounding environs for traces of the creature.

DID YOU KNOW?

In Greek mythology, Thetis was a sea nymph who lived in the Mediterranean and helped sailors during perilous storms.

SCANDALS, BOONDOGGLES AND WHITE ELEPHANTS

"In the Maritimes, politics is a disease, in Québec a religion, in Ontario a business, on the Prairies a protest and in British Columbia entertainment."

–Allan Fotheringham

There has been no shortage of political scandals and downright bizarre behaviour from the province's various elected officials over the years. Test your own knowledge of the wacky world of Left Coast politics with the following quiz.

1. One of the province's earliest premiers, former journalist Bill Smith, was famous for frequent fisticuffs, publicly bursting into tears and trying to hide the grey in his beard with shoe polish. Before moving to BC, what did he change his name to?
   - A) Smokey Smith
   - B) White Swan
   - C) Bif Naked
   - D) Amor De Cosmos
   - E) Nardwuar the Human Serviette

The answer is D. With a new name meaning "lover of the universe," Premier Amor De Cosmos ran the province from 1872 to 1874 and is considered by many to be one of the Fathers of Confederation.

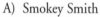

2. In 1888, Conservative Party member Edward Gawler Prior was elected to the House of Commons and became a cabinet minister for two different prime ministers before losing his seat for violating election rules. He turned to provincial politics and became premier in 1902, but he was fired by the lieutenant-governor the following year after awarding government contracts to his own private company. What major BC industry was Premier Prior involved with?

    A) Forestry
    B) Construction
    C) English as a second language
    D) Marijuana
    E) Whale watching

The answer is B. Suspicions were aroused after hardware company E.G. Prior received several construction contracts from E.G. Prior himself.

3. This BC premier purchased two primitive submarines from the Americans to help defend the coast in the unlikely event of a German attack during World War I.

    A) Theodore Davie
    B) Namor McKenzie
    C) Richard McBride
    D) Perry Scopes
    E) Arthur Curry

The answer is C. The subs bought by Premier McBride, affectionately known as "Handsome Dick" to his constituents, never saw any action and were sent to Halifax after the war, where they were promptly declared unfit for service and decommissioned.

4. What was the popular nickname given to William Andrew Cecil Bennett, who was premier from 1952 to 1972?
   A) King William
   B) Wacky
   C) The Wackster
   D) Billy the Kid
   E) Handsome Bill

The answer is B. W.A.C. Bennett's son, Bill Bennett, who was premier from 1975 to 1986, became known as Mini-Wac.

5. This BC premier was forced to resign after an apparent conflict of interest involving a botanical theme park, a Taiwanese entrepreneur and a mysterious $20,000 cash payment.
   A) Mike Harcourt
   B) Dan Miller
   C) Bill Vander Zalm
   D) Glen Clark
   E) Dave Barrett

The answer is C. Even though the ownership of Fantasy Gardens was in his wife's name, Premier Vander Zalm was found guilty in the court of public opinion for selling the money-losing theme park to a potential provincial investor. His Social Credit Party, despite being under new leadership, was obliterated in the next election.

6. After an auditor's report found that a former NDP finance minister had been skimming funds from Nanaimo charity bingo games for decades, Premier Mike Harcourt decided to "take a bullet for the party" and resigned from office even though he was not personally involved in the scandal. What was the name of the guilty party?

    A) Dave Stupid
    B) Dave Stupich
    C) Dave Gagliano
    D) Dave Snautier
    E) Dave Barrett

The answer is B. The "Bookkeeper" of Bingogate was later sentenced to two years' house arrest.

7. This BC premier was forced to resign after a contractor friend gave him a good deal on a new deck for his house instead of charging him union rates.
   A) John Hart
   B) William Bennett Sr.
   C) William Bennett Jr.
   D) Glen Clark
   E) Amor De Cosmos

The answer is D. Although the NDP leader was later acquitted of any wrongdoing, with the judge at the inquest saying there was "nothing in his conduct that crosses the line from an act of folly to behaviour calling for criminal sanctions," Clark never recovered politically from the live television broadcast of the RCMP raiding his home.

8. In 1995, the NDP government tried to revive the province's shipbuilding industry and commissioned the construction of three high-speed ferries. Because of various blunders, the cost of the program increased from the estimated $210 million to almost $460 million, and final delivery was almost three years behind schedule. Found to be suffering from numerous defects, the ferries were put up for sale and sold at an auction by the new Liberal government. How much were the vessels sold for?
   A) $200 million
   B) $100 million
   C) $50 million
   D) $19.5 million
   E) All the tea in China

The answer is D. Adding insult to injury, it was later revealed that the American buyers had offered the Liberals $60 million for the ferries prior to the auction.

9. This BC politician was arrested for drunk driving after being spotted weaving all over the road while vacationing in Maui.
   A) Nicholas Campbell
   B) Larry Campbell
   C) Kim Campbell
   D) Gordon Campbell
   E) Malcolm Lowry

The answer is D. Despite having a blood alcohol level of 0.149, nearly twice the legal limit, Premier Campbell was only given a $913 fine and a 90-day licence suspension.

10. Before being elected mayor, this Vancouver city councillor once helped an addict score some crack and let him smoke it in his van.
   A) Larry Campbell
   B) Jim Green
   C) Sam Sullivan
   D) Gilbert Sullivan
   E) Marion Berry

The answer is C. In his own defence, Mayor Sullivan said he was only trying to better understand the city's drug problems.

11. While answering a pre-arranged question, this member of Parliament for Vancouver once famously informed a startled House of Commons that, even as she was speaking, there were crosses burning on the lawns of Prince George.
    A) Jenny Kwan
    B) Nina Grewal
    C) Marg Delahunty
    D) Hedy Fry
    E) Libby Davies

The answer is D. No one in the northern BC community has seen a cross burning there, either as she was speaking or at any other time. Dr. Fry, who was then Minister of Multiculturalism, later made a statement expressing regret for her mistake about the specific racist activities in Prince George, leaving open the possibility that other unspecific hate crimes, perhaps off-lawn, were still flourishing.

12. When he was on the campaign trail in late 2000, Okanagan–Coquihalla MP and prime ministerial wannabe Stockwell Day, who once showed up to a press conference wearing a wet suit and riding a Jet Ski, promised voters he would hold a national referendum on any matter if 350,000 Canadians signed a petition requesting it. Comedian Rick Mercer responded with an online petition asking Canadians if they wanted the Alliance Party leader to change his name, which nearly one million people did. What would Stockwell Day's new name have been?
    A) Dean Stockwell
    B) Doris Day
    C) Doris von Kappelhoff
    D) Daniel Day-Lewis
    E) Stalker Day

The answer is B. Unlike Ms. von Kappelhoff, Mr. Day opted against changing his name to Doris Day.

13. Which of the following incidents is part of the colourful life story of former Burnaby NDP MP Svend Robinson?

A) Spending two weeks in jail after being arrested at an anti-logging protest

B) Travelling to the Middle East in an attempt to meet blockaded Palestinian leader Yasser Arafat

C) Suing the RCMP for shooting him in the leg with a rubber bullet

D) Surviving a fall off a 15-metre cliff

E) Stealing a $50,000 diamond ring for his boyfriend

F) All of the above

The answer is F. Love him or hate him, there has never been a Canadian politician quite like him.

14. A character from a popular television series was based on a former Vancouver coroner who became mayor. What is the fictional character's name?

A) Constable Constable

B) The Commish

C) Jed Bartlet

D) Cigarette-Smoking Man

E) Dominic Da Vinci

The answer is E. The lead character from Da Vinci's Inquest— *later* Da Vinci's City Hall—*followed Larry Campbell's career arc from policeman to chief coroner to mayor, but the show was mercifully cancelled before he could follow him to the Senate.*

BREAKING POLITICAL BARRIERS

Gaining Status

Canada's first First Nations person, and only the second aboriginal after Louis Riel, to be elected to a Canadian legislature was Frank Arthur Calder. Born in 1915 at Nass Harbour in northwestern BC, Calder is a member of the Nisga'a and was the first Native to graduate from the University of British Columbia. In 1949, he was elected MLA for the riding of Atlin and served off and on for 26 years. In 1972, he became Canada's first aboriginal cabinet minister but was dismissed the following year for disagreeing with NDP policy. He quit to join the Social Credit Party and was re-elected in 1975. His name is widely known because of the controversial Calder Case, which led to a landmark 1973 Supreme Court decision that dealt with Nisga'a land claims. He was named an officer of the Order of Canada in 1988.

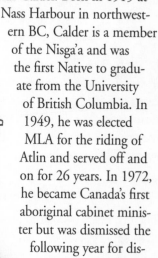

China Rises

After spending World War II with the Canadian Army fighting in the Far East, Victoria-born Douglas Jung became the first Chinese Canadian to be elected to the House of Commons. Jung was elected in 1957 as a Conservative for Vancouver Centre. During his term, he served as Canada's representative to the United Nations and helped establish both the Economic Council of Canada and the Canadian Coast Guard. He was named to the Order of Canada in 1990.

Winging It

In 1966, Peter Wing of Kamloops became the first Chinese mayor in North America after earning twice as many votes as the other two candidates put together. Mayor Wing's term was a big one for Kamloops; after the city joined with North Kamloops the following year, the province forced the amalgamation of the rest of the surrounding area, doubling the town's population.

Rosemary's Time

The first black woman to be elected to a legislature in Canada was Rosemary Brown, who won the Vancouver-Burrard riding for the NDP in 1972. She was re-elected in 1975 and ran for the leadership of the federal NDP the same year, while also raising three children. She lost on the fourth ballot to Ed Broadbent but set another first as the first woman to run for the leadership of a federal political party. Rosemary Brown retired from politics in 1986. Her autobiography, *Being Brown*, came out shortly after.

Trailer Park Gal

It's a long way to go from being a trailer park supervisor in Surrey to becoming BC's first female premier. After entering politics as a Surrey city councillor in 1969, Rita Johnston was elected to the legislature as a member of the Social Credit Party and later was appointed deputy premier by Bill Vander Zalm. When the

Fantasy Gardens scandal forced his resignation, she became acting premier on April 2, 1991. Formally elected party leader a few months later over frontrunner Grace McCarthy, she saw her party walloped in the polls by Mike Harcourt's NDP in October.

West Side Tory

Canada's first female prime minister was born in Port Alberni in 1947. Avril Phaedra Campbell, who gave herself the name Kim in her teens, was first elected to the House of Commons in 1988 as a Conservative. She served as Minister of Justice for several years before being transferred to the defence ministry by Prime Minister Brian Mulroney a month before he announced his retirement. After defeating Jean Charest for the party leadership, she officially became prime minister on June 25, 1993.

PM Miss

It was a short stay at 24 Sussex Drive. When Kim Campbell called an election in the fall, her party suffered the greatest defeat in Canadian political history. Only two Conservatives were elected in all of Canada (one of them was leadership rival Jean Charest), and Campbell lost her own Vancouver Centre seat to Liberal Hedy Fry. She left office after the third-shortest term as prime minister—only Sir Charles Tupper and John Turner were in power for less time. Although an infamous attack ad making fun of Liberal leader Jean Chrétien's facial paralysis didn't much help her campaign, the crushing defeat is considered more a rejection of the scandal-plagued Mulroney government than of Kim Campbell herself.

THE BEST GAME YOU CAN PLAY

The Puck Drops

The first hockey played in BC was between miners working in the Interior who had come from the East and brought the game with them. The Boundary Hockey League was born in 1908 with teams from Grand Forks, Phoenix and Greenwood.

Artificial Reality

The first BC hockey game played on artificial ice took place on January 3, 1912, when the New Westminster Royals outclassed the Victoria Aristocrats 8–3 in one of the first games of the Pacific Coast Hockey Association.

Early Roots of Western Alienation

The Aristocrats are best known for taking on the Québec Bulldogs for the Stanley Cup in 1913. The heavily favoured Québec team was expected to make an easy meal of the upstart Aristocrats but instead tied the first two games and lost 6–1 in the decisive third contest. Unfortunately for Victoria, the Stanley Cup board of trustees somehow decided the challenge wasn't "official," so the Bulldogs were able keep the trophy.

Who Wants to Beat the Millionaires?

Lord Stanley's Cup was first officially won by a team from BC two years later when the Vancouver Millionaires swept the sleepy Ottawa Senators in a best-of-five series. This was also the first series between the respective champions of the Pacific Coast Hockey Association (1911–24) and the National Hockey Association (1909–17).

Patron Saints

Home ice for the Millionaires was built by the wealthy Patrick family (Joe and sons Lester and Frank), the same lumber baron benefactors responsible for Victoria's first indoor rink. Located in Vancouver's West End, the Denman Arena was the world's largest ice rink and the second-largest sports building in North America after Madison Square Garden in New York.

Leading by Example

Frank Patrick was a player as well as an owner. The same year the Millionaires won the cup, he once scored six goals in a single game, a record for defencemen that stands to this day.

The Aristocats

The Aristocrats later changed their name to the Cougars, and in 1925, they took their revenge against Québec by beating the mighty Montréal Canadiens 3–1 in the finals. The Cougars were the last non-NHL team to hoist the Stanley Cup,

DID YOU KNOW?

When the Pacific Coast Hockey Association dissolved in 1926, the Cougars were relocated to Michigan and eventually became known as the Detroit Red Wings. So while it may be a stretch, truly desperate BC hockey fans can console themselves with the fact that one of their teams has actually won 10 Stanley Cups over the years.

Johnny-Come-Latelys

In 1970, the Vancouver Canucks became one of two new NHL expansion teams. Strangely, the Canucks were initially placed in the Eastern Division (allegedly to maintain parity between the two conferences), while the Chicago Black Hawks were placed in the West. The team's name is a homage to comic-book character Johnny Canuck, a World War II era, Nazi-battling cartoon superhero.

The Sport of Kings

The Canucks played their first game on October 9 against the Los Angeles Kings, losing 3–1 at the Pacific Coliseum. Their first victory, also on home ice, came two nights later when they defeated the Toronto Maple Leafs 5–3.

The First First Pick

Mel Bridgman of Victoria was the first BC hockey player to be a first-round NHL draft pick when the Philadelphia Flyers called his name in 1975. Bridgman scored 23 goals as a rookie, playing centre for Terry Crisp and Bob "Mad Dog" Kelly. He spent over six years in Philly, including the 1979–80 season, when the Broad Street Bullies set an NHL record, going undefeated in 35 consecutive games. After taking over as captain from Bobby Clarke, Bridgman was traded to the Calgary Flames in 1981 and ended his playing career as a member of the Canucks in 1988.

Rocked by Islanders

Led by Kevin McCarthy and Stan "the Steamer" Smyl, the Vancouver Canucks made it to the Stanley Cup finals for the first time in 1982. They were promptly swept by the New York Islanders, the Cup's defending champions.

 Canucks fans' custom of waving white towels began earlier in the 1982 playoff series, when coach Roger Neilson, frustrated by a series of crummy calls against his team, took a white trainer's towel, draped it over a spare stick and waved it in the air in mock surrender. Three players on the bench did the same, and all were subsequently ejected from the game. Thousands of spectators brought white towels with them to the next game, and a tradition was born.

Unmade in Manhattan

In 1994, the Canucks made their second and (to date) last appearance in the finals. Facing off against the New York Rangers, they made it all the way to Game 7 before a goal by future hall-of-famer Mark Messier ended Vancouver's hopes 3–2. Disgruntled fans went on one of the worst riots in Canadian history, causing millions of dollars in damage to Vancouver's downtown core. More than 100 people were arrested.

DID YOU  KNOW?

Mark Messier signed with the Canucks in 1997, taking over the captaincy from fan favourite Trevor Linden and spending three disappointing seasons in Vancouver before returning to Broadway as an unrestricted free agent.

Garage Hail

The Canucks played their first game in their new home, General Motors Place, aka "the Garage," on October 9, 1995. Mike Ridley scored Vancouver's first goal in their new digs, but the visiting Detroit Red Wings spoiled the housewarming party 5–3.

DID YOU  KNOW?

GM Place was the scene of the crime for the NHL's two longest suspensions. Former Wayne Gretzky bodyguard Marty McSorley of the Boston Bruins was given a 23-day suspension after whacking fellow enforcer Donald Brashear upside the head with his stick in March 2000. As the Bruins didn't make the playoffs, it effectively ended 37-year-old McSorley's playing career.

Canucks' star right winger Todd Bertuzzi received the second-longest and arguably the more severe sentence in March 2004 after sucker-punching Steve Moore of the Colorado Avalanche. Bertuzzi's punch was retaliation for Moore's dirty hit in an earlier game, which concussed Canucks captain Markus Naslund. Moore suffered three broken vertebrae in his neck after being driven to the ice. Bertuzzi was suspended for the 12 remaining regular-season games and the playoffs and was forbidden from playing elsewhere during the 2004–05 NHL lockout.

 BC BOASTS The men's gold-winning hockey team at the 2002 Winter Olympics in Salt Lake City featured five players born in BC: Eric Brewer (Vernon), Paul Kariya (Vancouver), Joe Sakic (Burnaby), Scott Niedermayer and Steve Yzerman (both from Cranbrook).

DOWNHILL ALL THE WAY

Norwegian Wood

While early Viking settlers in present-day Newfoundland were likely the first people to strap on skis in North America, it is their descendants, nearly 1000 years later, who are credited with bringing the sport to the continent. Scandinavian prospectors and miners who came to BC's Interior during the gold rushes of the mid-1800s used "Norwegian snowshoes" (as skis were then known) both as a means of transportation and for sport. Up to 4 metres long, the newfangled footwear quickly became popular in and around Revelstoke, a community with one of the highest annual snowfalls in the world. Local merchant F.B. Wells was the first to sell skis, and in 1891 he also helped establish the Revelstoke Ski Club, the country's oldest continuously operating ski club.

Jump Start

In the sport's early days, the primary emphasis was on catching huge air. From 1915 to the late 1960s, annual ski-jumping competitions were held on Mount Revelstoke. The length and natural grade of its 600-metre hill made jumps of over 60 metres possible, and over the years several world records were set at the site, which is still visible from downtown Revelstoke.

Red's Dawn

The first Canadian downhill ski championships were held at Red Mountain, near Rossland, in 1897. "Big Red" is one of the oldest ski resorts in North America, and in 1947, it was the first in BC to feature chairlifts. It hosted the first Canadian World Cup ski event, the du Maurier International, in 1968.

 Voted Canada's female athlete of the 20th century, Rossland's Nancy Greene, was the country's top ski racer through the 1960s, winning gold and silver medals at the 1968 Grenoble Olympics, as well as overall World Cup titles in 1967 and 1968. Her total of 13 World Cup victories is a Canadian record that stands to this day.

 Following her retirement from competition, Nancy Greene and her husband, Al Raine, were instrumental in the early development of Whistler-Blackcomb resort. In 1995, they moved to Kamloops to work similar magic with Sun Peaks Resort. She is free most winter days at 11:00 AM and 1:30 PM and can be found near the top of the Sunburst Express chair for anyone who would like to hit the slopes with her.

Must Be Something in the Water

In 1992, Kerrin Lee-Gartner, also from Rossland, capped a year with eight top 10 finishes on the World Cup circuit by winning a gold medal in downhill skiing at the Albertville Olympics. She was the first Canadian ever to win the event (Nancy Greene won her gold medal in the giant slalom).

Wild and Crazy Guys

Vancouverites Dave Murray and Steve Podborski were key members of the Crazy Canucks, a team of daredevil ski racers famous during the late 1970s both for their spectacular wipeouts and for record numbers of World Cup wins. Along with Dave Irwin and Ken Read, they won a total of 14 races and had dozens of top 10 placings. In 1982, Podborski became the first non-European to win the World Cup downhill trophy.

They Call Him Flipper

In 1975, Steve Corbett of Texada Island became the first person to complete a quadruple back flip on skis. Accomplished on Whistler Mountain, the feat was recorded in the film *In the Mind's Eye*—also notable for being the film debut of Vancouver character actor Bruce Greenwood (*Capote, Being Julia*), who did his own stunts while wearing a giant bunny suit.

Whistler's Sons

Ski racer Rob Boyd won three World Cup races and represented Canada in six world championships and three Olympic Games. His career highlight came in 1989 in front of a crowd in his hometown, Whistler, when he became the first Canadian male racer to win a World Cup downhill in his own country. The course on which he won, the "Dave Murray Downhill," is named in honour of the late Crazy Canucks team member.

Ross Rebagliati was the first athlete to win a gold medal for the sport of snowboarding at the 1998 Nagano Olympics. Three days later, the International Olympic Committee announced that he had tested positive for marijuana and stripped him of the medal. Rebagliati argued that the test results were caused by secondhand smoke from a going-away party held for him in Whistler, and the ruling was eventually overturned.

DID YOU KNOW?

The longest vertical descent in one day was recorded on April 20, 1998, when Tammy McMinn of Colorado successfully snowboarded down a slope near Atlin in the Alsek mountain range, 101 times. With help from Klondike Heliskiing, she made a total descent of roughly 373 kilometres in 14 hours and 50 minutes.

CANADIAN FOOTBALL

Lions Lore

The BC Lions played their first game in the Canadian Football League in 1954, losing 8–6 to the Winnipeg Blue Bombers. Early home games were held at Empire Stadium, which was demolished in 1984 and has been replaced by a soccer field at Hastings Park, home of the Pacific National Exhibition.

DID YOU  KNOW?

The football team's name was chosen after a contest was held in the local media. "The Lions" are distinctive twin peaks in the nearby North Shore mountains. According to local legend, they guard the city.

Cat Fights

The Lions won their first Grey Cup in 1964 and their second in 1985, both times playing against the Hamilton Tiger-Cats. They won again in 1994 against Baltimore (during a period when American teams briefly joined the CFL) and in 2000 against Montréal.

Legendary kicker Lui Passaglia spent his entire 23-year career (1976–99) with the Lions, setting a CFL record for playing the most games. He is pro football's all-time points leader and has kicked for more field goals (873), converts (1033) and punting yards (133,423) than anyone else in the annals of the game.

The Magic Flutie

Although his tenure in the Great White North lasted only eight years, NFL all-star Doug Flutie is widely considered one of the greatest quarterbacks to ever play Canadian football. In 1990, Flutie signed a two-year contract with the BC Lions. It made him the highest-paid player in the league ($350,000 per season), a paycheque he earned by setting the following CFL records: 730 pass attempts, 466 pass completions and 6619 thrown yards.

DID YOU KNOW?

Doug Flutie remains the only CFL player in history to have a breakfast cereal (Flutie Flakes) and a song ("Doug Flutie Song" by Moxy Früvous) named after him. He is the older brother of the CFL's all-time leader in catches, Darren Flutie.

ACTUAL FOOTBALL

Canadian Club

The sport of football, "the world's game," is known as soccer here in North America. Vancouver's professional team, founded in 1974, is officially known as the Whitecaps FC—an abbreviation for Football Club.

DID YOU KNOW?

The Whitecaps are named for both the nearby "white caps" of the North Shore mountains and the breaking waves of the Pacific Ocean. They play in the First Division of the United Soccer League, the largest system of soccer leagues in North America, at Swangard Stadium in Burnaby.

Bend It Like Bob

Vancouver-born midfielder Bob Lenarduzzi of the Whitecaps became the first Canadian to be named North American player of the year in 1978. He played for the team during its entire earlier incarnation (1974–84) and went on to become both the team's general manager and chairman.

Whitecaps on Top

In 1979, the Whitecaps beat the Tampa Bay Rowdies 2–1 in the Soccer Bowl finals held in New York City and became BC's first franchise to win a major North American championship. The team came home to the largest reception in provincial history (over 100,000 people), and midfielder Alan Ball was voted the league's MVP.

Known as the Vancouver Breakers until 2001, the Whitecaps Women became the first Canadian team to win the W-League title after a 4–2 penalty kick tiebreaker decision against the New Jersey Wildcats in 2004. Surrey-born defender Randee Hermus was voted the league's MVP. The men's team made the semifinals the same year.

AMERICA'S GAME

Opening Pitch

The first recorded baseball game in BC history took place at Barkerville in 1864. The game was organized by Thomas Pattullo, uncle of future premier Thomas Dufferin "Duff" Pattullo.

DID YOU  KNOW?

The first black player to appear on a baseball card was born in New Westminster in 1892. Jimmy Claxton, who moved to Tacoma, Washington, as a child, briefly played in the Pacific Coast League with the Oakland Oaks in 1916 before he was fired because of the colour of his skin.

Minor-League Canadians

The Vancouver Canadians are the farm team of the Oakland A's and one of the few successful minor-league baseball teams in Canada. The Canadians' team colours, ironically, are red, white and blue. They play home games at Nat Bailey Stadium next to scenic Queen Elizabeth Park.

Nat Bailey was the founder of the BC restaurant chain White Spot, which was the first drive-in restaurant in the country.

The Natural

Maple Ridge's Larry Walker is considered the best Canadian baseball player in the history of the game. Although, like most Canadian boys, he grew up wanting to be in the NHL, he was more at home on a diamond than on ice. As a member of the Colorado Rockies, the right fielder was named league MVP in 1997—the first and only Canuck to ever receive the award. The five-time all-star was awarded the Lou Marsh Trophy in 1998 and retired in 2005.

DID YOU KNOW?

Larry Walker's 409 total bases in 1997 set a new league record, though it has since been beaten by alleged steroid monkeys Barry Bonds and Sammy Sosa.

HOOP DREAMS

Bad News Bears

The Vancouver Grizzlies joined the National Basketball Association for the 1995–96 season as part of the league's two-pronged expansion into the Great White North (the Toronto Raptors also joined that year). Composed primarily of players taken from other teams via an expansion draft, the Grizzlies chose 213-centimetre-tall Bryant "Big Country" Reeves as their first-round pick. Coached by Stu Jackson, the team debuted with a pair of wins but had won only 13 more games by the end of the season. The Grizzlies established a grisly league record by losing 23 games in a row and finished the season as the lowest-ranked team in the NBA.

DID YOU  KNOW?

The team originally chose the name "Vancouver Mounties" but settled on Grizzlies after objections from the RCMP, who had recently signed over their licensing rights to the Disney Corporation in a five-year contract.

Going to Graceland

Sadly, the Vancouver Grizzlies were the worst team in NBA history. In 2001, owner Michael Heisley moved the franchise to Tennessee, where (now known as the Memphis Grizzlies) they quickly made a name for themselves as one of the league's better teams.

In 1996, the Phoenix Suns selected Steve Nash, a "short" 190-centimetre-tall point guard from Victoria, 15th overall in the first round of the NBA draft—the highest drafting ever of a Canadian player. Nine years later, he beat out superstar Shaquille O'Neal to be named the league's MVP, the first non-American to receive the honour and the first white guy in over 20 years. He then won the award a second time in 2006, becoming only the ninth player to win back-to-back MVP honours and only the second point guard to pull off the trick after Magic Johnson.

BRITISH COLUMBIAN GOLD

Man in Motion

In 1928, Percy Williams of Vancouver set a new world record by dashing 100 metres in 10.8 seconds at the Amsterdam Olympics. He also came first in the 200 metres and was the first Canadian to win two gold medals in track and field.

Columbian Strongman

Known today as the grandfather of modern power weightlifting, Vancouver's Douglas Hepburn won a gold medal in front of a home crowd at the British Empire Games in 1954. He had also won the world weightlifting championship in Sweden the previous year, despite having a sprained ankle.

Miracle Workers

Australian John Landy and Englishman Roger Bannister, at the time the only men in the world to have run a mile (1.6 kilometres) in under four minutes, competed against each other for the first time in a race at Vancouver's 1954 British Empire Games. It became known as the Miracle Mile and ended in a classic photo finish when Landy, in the lead, glanced over his left shoulder at the very instant Bannister passed him on the right. With a time of 3:58.8, Bannister won by 0.8 seconds, and both runners crossed the finish line in under four minutes. A statue commemorating the moment can be found today at Hastings Park, near where the race occurred.

DID YOU  KNOW?

The Miracle Mile was the first international sports event broadcast on live television and was also the lead story in the first issue of *Sports Illustrated* magazine.

Down Underdogs

In the Cinderella story of the 1956 Melbourne Olympics, a neophyte team of UBC rowers, none of whom had even sat in a rowing shell until the year before, won gold in the men's coxless four event. Lorne Loomer, Walter d'Hondt, Archie McKinnon and Don Arnold beat the American silver medalists by an impressive five boat lengths.

Nicknamed "Mighty Mouse" for her tiny build and her competitive mojo, Vancouver's Elaine Tanner is widely considered Canada's greatest female swimmer. During the 1966 Commonwealth Games in Kingston, Jamaica, 15-year-old Tanner won four gold medals and three silvers. That year she also became the youngest person to receive the Lou Marsh Trophy as Canada's top athlete. She won it again the following year after winning two golds and three silvers at the Pan Am Games in Winnipeg. She retired in 1968 after picking up "only" two silvers and a bronze at the Mexico City Olympics. A member of the Order of Canada, she remains the country's only female athlete in any sport to set four world records.

Ice Queen

Long-time national figure skating champion Karen Magnusson of North Vancouver won a gold medal at the 1973 worlds held in Bratislava, Czechoslovakia. She'd previously earned a silver at the Sapporo Olympics and was voted Canada's female athlete of the year in both 1971 and 1972.

Commanding Ten

On May 17, 1978, at the Edmonton Commonwealth Games, Victoria gymnast Philip Delasalle became the first Canadian gymnast to score a perfect 10 in an international competition. He went on to earn three more perfect scores in his best event, the pommel horse, over his career and introduced a trademark move known around the world as the "Delasalle."

Fung Coup

Vancouverite Lori Fung, who spent seven straight years as the national gymnastics grand champion, capped her career by winning the first gold medal ever awarded in rhythmic gymnastics at the 1984 Summer Olympics in Los Angeles.

Clean Sweeps

Linda Moore's North Vancouver Rec Centre rink won the 1985 women's world curling championship held in Sweden. It was the first time a BC rink had won an international curling competition, and also the first time the same country had won the championship two years in a row. Three years later, Moore skipped a team that won gold in women's curling, a demonstration sport at the Calgary Olympics.

World champion curler Rick Folk moved to Kelowna in the late 1980s and led his new BC team to a series of provincial and national wins. In 1994 his rink won 10 straight games in Oberstdorf, Germany, to take Canada's 22nd world title.

Rocking the Boat

BC-based rower Silken Laumann was the reigning world singles champion and the odds-on favourite to win gold at the 1992 Barcelona Olympics until her boat was accidentally rammed by a German rowing pair two months before the Games. Her leg was seriously injured. Within 10 days she underwent five operations, and her doctors said there was no way she could row in the Olympics.

Laumann staged a remarkable comeback, and with a specially fitted brace she was able to compete. Her bronze medal performance was one of the highlights of the games. Laumann was named Canada's female athlete of the year in 1991 and 1992 and won the Lou Marsh award in 1991 as Canada's outstanding athlete. She returned to competition in 1994, re-establishing herself as the best women's rower in the world, but suffered another setback at the Pan American Games in Argentina, when she was disqualified after testing positive for a drug contained in a common cold medication. She retired after winning a silver medal at the 1996 Atlanta Olympics.

Million-Dollar Lady

Dawn Coe-Jones of Lake Cowichan, BC, achieved eight top 10 finishes on the 1993 Ladies' Professional Golf Association tour, becoming the first Canadian woman golfer to win one million bucks in prize money.

The Fury out of Surrey

In 1999, Simon Fraser University student Daniel Igali won a gold medal at the world wrestling championships in Ankara, Turkey, in the 69-kilogram freestyle category. As an encore, he won another gold medal in the same weight class at the Sydney Olympics the following year.

DID YOU KNOW?

Igali was born in Nigeria but applied for refugee status in Canada after competing in the 1994 Commonwealth Games in Victoria. He ran as the Surrey-Newton candidate for the BC Liberal Party in the 2005 provincial election, but his success in the ring didn't translate to the political arena, and he was soundly beaten by New Democrat Harry Bains.

Victoria's Secret Weapon

The Garden City is becoming known for producing some of the fastest cyclists on the planet:

- University of Victoria graduate Alison Sydor won Canada's first medal (a bronze) in women's world championship road racing in 1991. She also won a silver medal in the inaugural cross-country mountain biking event at the 1996 Atlanta Olympics and four world championship gold medals in the same discipline.

- Victoria-based triathlete Simon Whitfield's gold medal win at the 2000 Sydney Olympics was one of the most memorable performances by an individual athlete in Canadian sporting history. Whitfield picked himself up after he and 14 other riders wiped out in the cycling portion of the event, and he worked his way back to the front of the pack. His final overall time was 1:48:24.02, which still stands as the fastest Olympic triathlon.

- Between 2001 and 2002, Victoria resident Roland Green became a two-time world mountain bike champion and the first-ever Commonwealth Games mountain bike champ.

- Sam Whittingham of Victoria set a new cycling speed record at the 2001 World Human Powered Speed Challenge in Nevada. He was clocked at 130 kilometres per hour. His wife, Andrea Blaseckie, holds the women's record with a speed of 88 kilometres per hour.

BC RECORDS

Terminal City Velocity

On May 24, 1912, Charles Saunders made history as the first Canadian to jump out of a perfectly good airplane. After sitting just behind the pilot's seat as the plane took off from Hastings Park in East Vancouver, he hung by his hands under the plane until it reached an altitude of 300 metres. His parachute, held in a makeshift metal container above the plane's skids, was deployed by tilting the plane up at a 45-degree angle and spilling the parachute off the back of the skids. Saunders dropped about 40 metres before his chute opened. The jump was the third in the world from an airplane and only the second that was not fatal.

Wheelbarrow Positioning

Richmond's Brian Rhodes and John Cortes set a new record for the fastest time for a one-mile (1.6-kilometre) wheelbarrow race at the Ladner Centennial Sports Festival in Delta in 1980. The two speedsters crossed the finish line in just 4 minutes and 52 seconds.

The Seven-Summit Itch

In 1982, Invermere-raised Patrick Morrow became the first person from BC to summit Mount Everest and only the second Canadian (teammate Laurie Skreslet was first) to do so. Realizing he'd already stood on the highest points in Africa (Kenya's Mount Kilimanjaro), North America (Alaska's Denali/Mount McKinley) and South America (Argentina's Aconcagua), Morrow decided to go for a grand slam and climb the highest peaks of the remaining continents as well. He went on to summit Antarctica's Vinson Massif in 1985, Oceania's Carstensz Pyramid in 1986 and finished with Europe's Mount Elbrus in the Caucasus range later the same year. American businessman Dick Bass had claimed the feat before him, but while Bass used Australia's wee Mount Kosciusko as one of his seven targets, Morrow included all of Oceania in his continental definition—Carstensz Pyramid in Irian Jaya is nearly twice Kosciusko's size. He was made a member of the Order of Canada in 1987.

Grouse Grinders

After spending 83 hours and 17 minutes on the slopes, Vancouver's Dave Phillips and Garry O'Neil set a new world record for non-stop skiing in February 1986 at Grouse Mountain.

The Big Waterski

Not content with holding the longest non-stop alpine skiing record, Dave Phillips, along with new partner Ralph Hildebrand, set a new record for waterskiing eight years later on North Vancouver's Indian Arm. The duo covered roughly 2150 kilometres over 56 hours and 35 minutes, using infrared binoculars and spotlights to stay on the course at night.

Fin Swim

In order to draw attention to pollution in the Fraser River, one of the largest salmon-producing rivers in the world, intrepid

Coquitlam city councillor Fin Donnelly donned a life jacket, wetsuit and flippers and swam the entire 1399-kilometre length of the Fraser over 21 days in September 1995.

DID YOU KNOW?

Aqua enthusiast Donnelly is the executive director of the Rivershed Society of British Columbia, a non-profit charity advocating sustainable living in the Fraser River Basin, where most of BC's population resides. Donnelly swam 3200 kilometres of BC's rivers, lakes and ocean and set speed records for swimming the Strait of Juan De Fuca (10 hours, 10 minutes) and Georgia Strait (8 hours, 5 minutes).

Amazon Warrior

Colin Angus of Port Alberni gets around. In 1999, with no major sponsorship, no high-end gear, no support team and very little whitewater experience, he and two others became the first people to raft the entire length of the mighty Amazon River. After an inauspicious start, in which they all nearly died of dehydration and altitude sickness before they even reached the source of the river high in the Peruvian Andes, they put their inflatable boat in the water and somehow managed to survive the raging Class 5 rapids, lack of food and clean water, and trigger-happy Shining Path guerrillas to complete the 64,000-kilometre expedition to the river's mouth in the Atlantic.

Colin Angus's latest venture is to be the first person to circumnavigate the globe using only human power. After setting off from Vancouver on June 1, 2004, in a rowboat headed for Russia, Angus has since cycled, walked, paddled and even crawled a good chunk of the 42,000-kilometre journey. As this book went to press, he was cycling north from Costa Rica after rowing across the Atlantic with his fiancée, Julie Wafaei, whom he met en route.

GREAT CANADIANS

In May 2004, over one million Canadians took part in a CBC contest to name the 100 greatest Canadians of all time. Of the finalists, eight came from BC, and two of them made the top 10. And the BC winners are:

#90: BRYAN ADAMS

This raspy-voiced rock star is famous around the world for both his blue-collar stadium anthems and his syrupy soundtrack ballads. Born in Kingston, Ontario, but raised in Vancouver, Adams co-wrote the Canadian famine-relief single "Tears Are Not Enough" and has been cranking out hit albums for over two decades. His 1991 single "Everything I Do (I Do It for You)," from the soundtrack for *Robin Hood: Prince of Thieves*, went to number one in several countries and sat at the top of the charts for a record-setting 16 weeks. Currently forging a second career as a photographer, he has been inducted into Canada's Walk of Fame and in 1998 was named an officer of the Order of Canada.

Adams came in behind the fastest man alive, Donovan Bailey, but received more votes than reform-minded federal politician Preston Manning.

DID YOU KNOW?

One of Adams' earliest hits was "Summer of '69," a nostalgic ode to the best days of his life, when he spent his evenings down by the drive-in and had a band who tried real hard. Young Bryan was actually only nine years old that year.

Adams has a thing about old buildings. He was one of the more vocal critics of the decision to knock down Vancouver's art deco Georgia Medical Building in the 1980s, and he later bought and refurbished the Oppenheimer Brothers Warehouse in Gastown. Named after the city's second mayor, David Oppenheimer, and his brothers, the structure is one of the city's oldest buildings and now houses a state-of-the-art recording studio where artists such as Metallica, Elton John, Nine Inch Nails and REM have recorded albums.

#85: Emily Carr

More than half a century after her death, artist Emily Carr has become a Canadian icon, familiar even to people who know nothing about art. She was born in Victoria in 1871 and moved to San Francisco to study art at age 20 after the death of her parents. After completing further studies in Europe, she returned home in 1911 where, fascinated by the First Nations cultures of the Pacific Northwest, she travelled up and down the coast, painting Native villages and totem poles. She soon amassed a large portfolio of work but was unable to find any buyers, which caused her to give up painting for many years. To make a living, she ran a small apartment house in Victoria.

The period of work on which Carr's reputation rests today didn't begin until she was already 57 years old. An ethnologist working at UBC stumbled across some of her early paintings and sent them to the curator of the National Gallery of Canada, who at the time was organizing an exhibition of West Coast Native art. He asked to include some of Carr's work in the show and sent her a train ticket to Ottawa for the opening. While in the East, she met members of the famous Group of Seven, who encouraged her to return to her easel. Her focus on Native culture and totem poles alone was soon complemented by expressive paintings of BC's forests, driftwood-strewn beaches and expansive skies.

The reclusive West Coast painter didn't receive as many points as gold-medal-winning figure skater Kurt Browning, but she received a better score than golfer Mike Weir.

Klee Wyck is the nickname given to Emily Carr by the Nuu-chah-nulth of Vancouver Island. It translates as "the laughing one." Neighbours in Victoria, on the other hand, referred to her as "crazy old Millie."

DID YOU KNOW?

Emily Carr loved animals and had a menagerie of critters at her Victoria boarding house, including an albino rat, a parrot, several dogs and a monkey that she often wheeled about town in a baby carriage.

#80: Chief Dan George

The late Chief Dan George is Canada's most famous First Nations leader and is often credited with helping to usher in a new era of Native pride. Born Geswanouth Slahoot on a reserve in North Vancouver in 1899, his name was officially changed when he entered a residential school at the age of five. George worked at a variety of jobs including longshoreman, construction worker, musician and school bus driver before becoming chief of the Tsleil-waututh (Burrard band) in 1951.

When he was in his 60s, he was bitten by the acting bug and landed a part in the CBC television series *Cariboo Country*. He performed the same role in *Smith*, a Disney movie adapted from the series in 1969. His first big break as an actor came when he was cast as Old Lodge Skins in the 1970 film *Little Big Man*, a role for which the untrained actor received an Oscar nomination for best supporting actor. Another career highlight came when he starred opposite Clint Eastwood in the classic western *The Outlaw Josey Wales*.

Chief Dan George didn't put up the same numbers as puck-stopper Ed "the Eagle" Belfour, but he scored higher than curling champion Sandra Schmirler.

DID YOU KNOW?

Arthur Penn, the director of *Little Big Man*, initially offered the role of Chief Old Lodge Skins to Marlon Brando, who turned him down to play Don Corleone instead.

#75: SARAH McLACHLAN

A former busker from the Maritimes, this singer-songwriter and West Vancouver resident has gone on to become one of Canada's greatest and most distinctive musical talents. Thanks to her pivotal role in the women-only Lilith Fair travelling music festival, which raised over $7 million for charity, the breathy soprano has moved from fringe-dwelling Canadian folkie to a major mainstream recording artist. She has sold over 25 million records worldwide, won three Grammy awards and received both the Order of Canada and a private audience with the Pope. McLachlan has also lent her voice to many social causes—cancer research and the plight of jailed Native leader Leonard Peltier in particular—and founded the Sarah McLachlan Music Outreach Program to provide free music classes to inner-city students whose school music programs have been axed by budget cuts.

Sarah didn't get as many votes as Emily Murphy, Canada's first female judge and a key player in getting women the right to vote, but she received more than Lieutenant Colonel John McRae, the "In Flanders Field" poet from World War I.

#51: PAMELA ANDERSON

One of the more eyebrow-raising inductees to the list of greatest Canadians is oft-naked model/actress Pamela Anderson. This Ladysmith local received her big break when a cameraman beamed her image onto BC Place Stadium's Jumbotron at a BC Lions football game in 1989. The crowd went wild at the sight of the buxom beauty wearing a Labatt's Blue t-shirt, and the rest is history. The brewery promptly hired her to promote its wares, a modelling gig that led to her becoming a "Tool Time" girl on the *Home Improvement* sitcom, *Playboy* model, *Baywatch* babe, pole-dancing instructor, PETA spokesperson, magazine columnist and, last but not least, the most internationally recognizable Canadian of all time. In April 2006, she hosted the Juno Award ceremony held in Halifax.

Located near the middle of the list, the stacked actress is sandwiched between comedian Rick Mercer and international children's rights activist Craig Kielburger.

 As the first baby born on July 1, 1967, the 100th anniversary of Confederation, young Pam won early fame as Canada's "Centennial Baby."

DID YOU KNOW?

NBC cancelled *Baywatch*, her TV series about an attractive group of lifeguards in sunny California, after its first season. Resuscitated two years later, it went on to become one of the most popular shows in history—broadcast in 148 countries and on every continent except Antarctica. It ran for 11 seasons (1989–2001) and has the dubious distinction of being the longest-running series never to win an Emmy award.

#32: Michael J. Fox

Actor Michael Andrew Fox grew up in the Vancouver suburb of Burnaby. In order to avoid being confused with film star Michael Fox (*Machine-Gun Kelly*, *Whatever Happened to Baby Jane?*), he adopted the "J." as a tribute to character actor Michael J. Pollard (*Bonnie and Clyde*, *Tango and Cash*). The perennially boyish thespian's first role came at the age of 15 playing a 10-year-old in the short-lived CBC sitcom *Leo and Me*. Although an accomplished dramatic actor, Fox is best known for comedic roles such as *Family Ties'* budding Republican Alex P. Keaton, time-travelling teenager Marty McFly in the *Back to the Future* trilogy, and New York deputy mayor Mike Flaherty in *Spin City*.

Fox has also written a book, *Lucky Man*, about his life and his experience with Parkinson's disease. He was diagnosed with the disease in 1991, but kept the information private for seven years. He has since become a strong supporter of stem cell research, which he believes may one day help sufferers of this and other debilitating illnesses.

Michael J. Fox ranks behind iconic author Pierre Berton but ahead of melancholic minstrel Gordon Lightfoot.

DID YOU  KNOW?

While the causes of Parkinson's remain unclear, scientists are studying whether environmental toxins play a part. Of *Leo and Me*'s 125-member cast and crew, four have since been diagnosed with Parkinson's, an improbably high percentage. Although an individual's genes play a factor, studies have found there is an increased risk of the disease among certain occupations such as hospital workers, loggers and miners.

#5: DAVID SUZUKI

Renowned geneticist and broadcaster Dr. David Suzuki is a one-man environmental movement. As the host of the popular CBC program *The Nature of Things* and the author of over 30 books, he has earned worldwide renown as an advocate of sustainable ecology. His accessible science and sense of humour have made him a household name.

Suzuki, a third-generation Japanese Canadian, was born in Vancouver in 1936. When he was six years old, he and his sisters (none of whom spoke Japanese) and mother were placed in an internment camp near Slocan with other Japanese families after the bombing of Pearl Harbor. His father was sent to a labour camp in Solsqua, BC.

He first made a name for himself as a scientist in 1969 after becoming a professor of zoology at the University of British Columbia. With the aim of controlling pests, he conducted genetic research on the common fruit fly and ended up being able to breed a strain of fly that died in hot weather. This was significant not only because of its use for pest control, but also because it meant that scientists could examine similar defects to probe the development and behaviour of insects.

A natural in front of the camera, Suzuki made the move to national broadcasting in 1971 as host of the weekly CBC TV show *Suzuki on Science*. He later created CBC Radio's *Quirks and Quarks* before beginning his stint hosting *The Nature of Things*.

In 1990, he founded the David Suzuki Foundation to help promote sustainability.

The good doctor was bested by insulin co-founder Frederick Banting, but did better at the polls than former prime minister Lester Pearson. His own vote, incidentally, was for Tommy Douglas.

#2: TERRY FOX

In 1977, Port Coquitlam athlete Terry Fox was an 18-year-old kinesiology student at Simon Fraser University when he was diagnosed with bone cancer that resulted in the amputation of his right leg 15 centimetres above the knee. After undergoing chemotherapy and seeing other people, particularly children, suffering with cancer, he decided to do something to help find a cure. Terry came up with the idea of a "Marathon of Hope"—a run across Canada to raise money and generate publicity for cancer research. His goal was to raise one dollar from every Canadian to help find a cure. In St. John's, Newfoundland, on April 12, 1980, he dipped his artificial leg in the Atlantic and began the run. He ran nearly 43 kilometres a day for 143 days, but by September the cancer had returned, and he was forced to stop in Thunder Bay, Ontario.

Terry Fox died 10 months later, but by then his dream had been realized, and over $24 million had been collected in his name. That September, the first Terry Fox Run was held, and the annual international charity event has since raised $360 million dollars for cancer research.

Fox didn't garner quite as many votes as the overall winner, Tommy Douglas, but he managed to outdistance flamboyant former prime minister Pierre Trudeau.

 While Terry Fox is a heroic figure known around the world, another, lesser-known, young British Columbian who lost a leg to cancer completed Fox's run just a few years later. Steve Fonyo followed in his friend's footsteps, starting his "Journey for Lives" on March 31, 1984, and ending it 7924 kilometres later at what is now known as Steve Fonyo Beach in Victoria. He received less publicity and support at first, but emerged from Fox's shadow after passing beyond the symbolic point outside Thunder Bay where his predecessor was forced to quit. Fonyo raised $13 million for cancer research and was appointed to the Order of Canada in 1987.

Not to be outdone by the one-legged Fox and Fonyo, Rick Hansen, a paraplegic athlete from Port Alberni, opted to circumnavigate the globe in a wheelchair to raise public awareness of and funds for spinal cord research. Hansen's "Man in Motion World Tour" began from Vancouver's Oakridge shopping mall on March 21, 1985. He went on to roll through 34 countries, four continents, five mountain ranges and even a flood while wearing out five wheelchairs, 80 pairs of gloves and over 100 tires in the process. Hansen finally made it back to Vancouver 26 months later, and 7000 spectators greeted him in a welcome-home ceremony that was broadcast live across the country. Of the $14 million the marathon raised, all but $28,000 came from Canadians.

Among the thousands of people Rick Hansen inspired was Salish artist Corey Baines, who included his likeness on a totem pole located in the city of Duncan on Vancouver Island.

THE COUNTRY'S WESTERN MUSIC

Living in Harmony

One of the first musicians from BC to hit the big time was one half of the husband-and-wife folk duo known as Ian and Sylvia. Ian Tyson was born in Victoria in 1933 and only learned to play guitar after injuries from a fall ended his dreams of becoming a rodeo star. He relocated to Toronto in the hopes of earning a living through music, and it was there he met Sylvia Fricker. After Bob Dylan's manger discovered them playing the New York coffee-house circuit in 1962, the couple went on to make 10 albums together, becoming one of Canada's most successful recording acts with original songs and covering music by Joni Mitchell and Gordon Lightfoot. In 1994, they were both made members of the Order of Canada.

DID YOU KNOW?

A CBC poll in 2005 determined Ian Tyson's song "Four Strong Winds" to be the "most essential" piece of Canadian music ever. Ian wrote the song after hearing his friend Bob Dylan play "Blowing in the Wind" for the first time in front of an audience.

Taylor-Made Soul

Bobby Taylor & the Vancouvers were, as you've probably guessed, originally from Vancouver. The soul band signed with Motown Records and had a big hit with the song "Does Your Mother Know About Me?" in 1964. Taylor is best known, however, for his work as a producer and is credited with discovering the Jackson 5. Taylor brought the group to Motown after the teenage quintet opened for a Vancouvers concert, and he also produced their first recordings, including their cover of the Miracles' "Who's Lovin' You."

 DID YOU KNOW?

Other famous members of the Vancouvers included Tommy Chong (one half of stoner comedy duo Cheech and Chong) and, briefly, a teenaged future guitar god named Jimi Hendrix, whose father and grandparents lived in Vancouver.

A Hard Day's Flight

On August 22, 1964, the Beatles played to a sold-out house at Vancouver's old Empire Stadium, but the historic show almost didn't take place. After playing in Seattle, the Fab Four hopped into a rented jet and headed north, but as they neared the border they were denied permission to land. In all the chaos of Beatlemania, they'd forgotten to clear U.S. customs. The pilot turned the plane around and headed back to Sea-Tac Airport, where they completed inspection in about 20 minutes and made it to Vancouver just in time.

At a time when the pop charts were dominated by Ringo Starr and his bandmates, Lucille Starr of Coquitlam had a huge international hit with "The French Song." Sung in Canada's two official languages, the 1964 ballad was produced by Herb Alpert with his famous Tijuana Brass playing backup, and it became the first recording by a Canadian artist to sell a million copies. Starr's other hits during the 1960s included "Yours," "Crazy Arms," "Jolie Jaqueline" and "Bonjour Tristesse." A street in Coquitlam, Lucille Starr Drive, is named in her honour.

Lucille is actually the one doing Cousin Pearl's famous yodelling on the hit TV series *The Beverly Hillbillies*.

Hell Raisers

Since it has sold 6 million copies, it's a good guess that one in every five Canadian households has a copy of *Hot Shots*, Trooper's greatest hits collection, hidden away somewhere. Giving the Rolling Stones a run for their money as the world's oldest rock band, the members of Trooper have been playing together since their Vancouver high-school days in the mid-1960s, and crowds still clamour to hear time-tested classics such as "We're Here for a Good Time," "Raise a Little Hell," "Round Round We Go" and "The Boys in the Bright White Sports Car." Any bar in Canada big enough to have a stage has probably seen Trooper raise a little hell on it at one time or another.

Been Gone, Gone, Gone So Long

It is safe to say that Chilliwack is probably the only band with a Coast Salish name to hit Billboard's Top 40. Initially called the Classics and then the Collectors before finally settling on Chilliwack (a term meaning "going back up" as well as being the name of a small Fraser Valley city), the Vancouver band has released 13 albums since its 1970 debut and has hit the charts with singles such as "Fly At Night" (not to be confused with Rush's "Fly By Night"), "I Believe," "My Girl (Gone, Gone, Gone)" and "Whatcha Gonna Do." Hugely popular and with a devoted hippie fan base, the band was often referred to as Canada's answer to the Grateful Dead.

He Had Joy, He Had Fun

It's been a long time since "Seasons in the Sun" became a monster hit for Vancouverite Terry Jacks, but the syrupy 1974 single is still among the all-time bestsellers issued by a Canadian artist. It spent more than three months on the charts and sold 11.5 million copies worldwide. Jacks decided to cover the Jacques Brel song after a close friend died of leukemia.

School of Rock

One of the new millennium's unlikelier musical success stories is the Langley Schools Music Project. In the late 1970s, long-haired roadhouse rocker Hans Fenger began teaching music classes in the Lower Mainland farming community of Langley. After teaching his prepubescent choir about the three Bs (Beach Boys, Beatles and Bowie) and equipping them with electric bass, bare-bones percussion and a xylophone, he herded them into the school gymnasium to make a recording, copies of which were distributed to the students and their loved ones.

 Decades later, a copy of the low-budget recording somehow made its way to the desk of radio deejay Irwin Chusid. He convinced Bar/None Records to re-release it as a limited edition, and the one-of-a-kind recording immediately created an international buzz, making many end-of-the-year best album lists in 2001. The kids' interpretations of pop hits du jour run from Froot Loop–fuelled frenzies ("Good Vibrations," "I'm Into Something Good") to mournful dirges ("Desperado," "Calling Occupants of Interplanetary Craft"), lending the songs a power that even their originators couldn't achieve. As David Bowie himself describes their cover of his song "Space Oddity": "The backing arrangement is astounding. Coupled with the earnest if lugubrious vocal performance, you have a piece of art that I couldn't have conceived of, even with half of Colombia's finest export products in me."

Anarchy in BC

Touring virtually nonstop since their 1978 debut, Vancouver trio D.O.A. helped spearhead the spread of punk rock counterculture around the world. They made the term "hardcore" a household word with their legendary album *Hardcore 81* and perennial crowd-pleaser "Disco Sucks" squeaked in at number 49 on the CBC's list of the 50 greatest Canadian songs. Having played benefit concerts for over 100 different causes, they are the world's oldest punk band still standing, and Vancouver mayor Larry Campbell declared December 21, 2003, to be "D.O.A. Day" in their honour.

Under Foster's Care

The city of Richmond is home to David Foster, one of the most successful composers in modern history. Foster almost single-handedly invented the Top 40 genre known as "adult contemporary" by writing and producing hits for the likes of Chicago, Lionel Richie, Michael Jackson, Whitney Houston and Celine Dion. Since 1979, he has been nominated for 38 Grammy awards, won 14, and received a President's Merit award in 1998. Standout tracks include the number one singles "St. Elmo's Fire" (also the theme music for Rick Hansen's Man In Motion tour) and "Tears Are Not Enough," the famine-relief anthem he co-wrote with Bryan Adams and Jim Vallance. The indefatigable soft-rock songwriter's latest protégé is chart-topping former wedding singer Michael Bublé of Burnaby.

Trusted by Millions

On the day John Lennon was murdered, three teenaged Vancouverites played their very first gig in front of a small crowd at the city's now-defunct Smiling Buddha Cabaret. Their set comprised just six original tunes—played four times each—and they took requests from a depressed crowd of about 15. Since then, 54-40 has gone on to become one of the biggest bands in Canada with such songs as "One Day in Your Life," "Ocean Pearl" and "She-La." Although they never caught on below the border, their song "I Go Blind" was a huge hit for American frat-house favourites Hootie & the Blowfish.

DID YOU KNOW?

In the 1840s, the slogan of American expansionists was "Fifty-four Forty or Fight!" a battle cry demanding the boundary line between Oregon and the Canadian Northwest run through the location of present-day Prince Rupert. Fortunately, President James Polk reached a compromise with England and the border was established at the 49th parallel rather than at 54°40'.

Thriller Nights

The biggest concert in BC music history took place when not-yet-disgraced moonwalker Michael Jackson came to town for three shows in November 1984. Total attendance for the three concerts was about 110,000.

Don't Care too Much for Money

BC billionaire Jim Pattison set a new record in 1985 for the highest amount paid for pop music memorabilia when he forked out over $2.2 million for John Lennon's psychedelic 1965 Phantom V Rolls Royce.

Orchestral Manoeuvres as a Lark

The largest orchestra in history played together at BC Place on May 15, 2000. A grand total of 6452 musicians, made up of members of the Vancouver Symphony Orchestra and music students from throughout the province, played Beethoven's "Ode to Joy" and "O Canada."

Appetite for Destruction

One of the worst riots in Canadian history took place on November 7, 2002, when Guns N' Roses failed to show up for their gig at GM Place, which would have been the start of the band's first North American tour in a decade. Fans showed their displeasure by smashing venue windows, overturning barricades and throwing rocks at the police, who responded by pepper-spraying and clubbing anyone within range, including several innocent bystanders. Damages were estimated at over $350,000, and 12 people were arrested.

Nanaimo Star

Inspired by such jazz luminaries as Nat King Cole and Fats Weller, Nanaimo-born pianist Diana Krall shot to fame singing the same standards her idols did. Not long after her professional debut, playing in local restaurants at age 15, she won a Vancouver Jazz Festival scholarship to the prestigious Berklee College of Music in Boston.

The sultry-voiced singer's single "When I Look In Your Eyes" won a Grammy award for best jazz vocal performance in 1999, and *Live in Paris* earned her another for best jazz album three years later. Krall received an honorary PhD in fine arts from the University of Victoria in 2003, and she was made an officer of the Order of Canada in 2005.

Huge Chunk of Change

Vancouver's platinum-selling grunge-lite rockers Nickelback saw three singles ("How You Remind Me," "Too Bad," "Never Again") from their fourth album, *Silver Side Up*, hit number one on the Billboard charts. They also hit the top with "Figured You Out" from 2003's *The Long Road* and "Photograph" from the *All the Right Reasons* album in 2005.

 The nouveau riche foursome's name comes from singer Chad Kroeger's former life working at Starbucks, where he was constantly giving a nickel in change back to customers.

DID YOU  KNOW?

Silver Side Up was released on September 11, 2001. The band was on the tour bus that morning, driving across Pennsylvania just a few miles from where United Airlines Flight 93 hit the ground.

Fly Girl

In 2002, the first single from 20-year-old songbird Nelly Furtado's first album, *Whoa Nelly,* won a Grammy award. The Victoria musician was also nominated in three other categories. "I'm Like A Bird" was voted song of the year, while the follow-up single, "Turn Off the Lights," went to number one on Billboard's dance charts. Her 2006 album *Loose* also flew to the top of the charts with its first two singles "Promiscuous" and "Maneater" both reaching the number one spot.

 The daughter of working-class Portuguese immigrant parents, Nelly spent eight summers as a teenager working alongside her mother as a chambermaid at Victoria's Robin Hood Hotel before hitting the big time.

Some Songs That Mention British Columbia

"This Land Is Your Land"—The Travellers, 1955

"Summer Wages"—Ian & Sylvia, 1966

"The Lumberjack Song"—Monty Python, 1970

"The Living Garbage Truck"—Frank Zappa & the Mothers of Invention, 1970

"My Uncle"—Flying Burrito Brothers, 1972

"Vancouver Shakedown"—Nazareth, 1976

"Vancouver"—Genesis, 1978

"Life is a Highway"—Tom Cochrane, 1991

"Knockin' On Mine"—Paul Westerberg, 1993

"Vancouver"—Violent Femmes, 1993

"Maps of the World"—John Cale, 1994

"Smoke the Sky"— Mötley Crüe, 1994

"Heartbeat"—KRS-One, 1997

"Canadian Rose"—Blues Traveler, 1997

"Heart Cooks Brain"—Modest Mouse, 1997

"Severe Punishment"—Wu Tang Clan, 1997

"Clockwork"—The Rascalz, 1997

"Vancouver"—Jeff Buckley, 1998

"You Never Know"—Hieroglyphics, 1998

"Surfing in Tofino"—The Planet Smashers, 1999

"Beautiful Day"—Len, 1999

"Counter Parts"—Swollen Members, 1999

"Peace Not Greed"—Kottonmouth Kings, 2000

"Worldwide"—Outlawz, 2000

"Vancouver Divorce"—Gordon Downie, 2001

"NBA"—Joe Budden, 2003

BC LETTERS

Under the North Shore Mountains

Far and away the most famous book ever written in BC is
Under the Volcano, a novel by bibulous British author Malcolm
Lowry, who moved to the Vancouver area in 1939. Set in
Mexico on the Day of the Dead (though it includes a reference
to the author's new home province as a "genteel Siberia"),
Lowry's tale of a doomed, drunken former British consul on the
eve of World War II was mostly written in a squatter's shack near
present-day Cates Park in North Vancouver. The book was
declared a masterpiece when it was published in 1947, and
Lowry's semi-autobiographical main character, Geoffrey Firmer,
was hailed as the definitive anti-hero of the times.

Although the city constantly tried to evict the alcoholic author
from his beach shack on Burrard Inlet over the 14 years he spent
there, today the site where he lived is marked with a plaque, and
a trail called "Malcolm Lowry Walk" runs along the waterfront.

DID YOU  KNOW?

Albert Finney received a best actor Oscar nomination for his performance in a 1984 film based on the book.

 Under the Volcano is also the name of Vancouver
recording duo Rock & Hyde's 1987 debut album,
which spawned the minor hits "Dirty Water" and
"I Will."

Rule's Attraction

In a strange twist to academia's usual "publish or perish" dictum, UBC English professor Jane Rule's first novel, *Desert of the Heart*, almost cost the writer her job when it came out in 1964. Homosexuality was still illegal at the time, and her book about two women who fall for each other in Reno, Nevada, is considered to be one of literature's first unambiguous lesbian love stories. *Desert Hearts*, a film based on the novel, starring Helen Shaver and Patricia Charbonneau, came out in 1985. Rule was inducted into the Order of British Columbia in 1998.

Copper Tops

Since it was first published in 1981, *Daughters of Copper Woman* has become an underground classic, selling over 200,000 copies. Now in its 13th reprinting, Anne Cameron's feminist retelling of Native legends passed on to her by Nuu-chah-nulth and Coast Salish women is the bestselling work of fiction about British Columbia by someone born here.

A Cornfield of their Own

Although he is the author of over 30 books, as well as hundreds of short stories and screenplays, Chilliwack writer W.P. Kinsella is best known for his 1980 novel *Shoeless Joe*, upon which Kevin Costner based his movie *Field of Dreams*. The film's catchphrase, "If you build it, he will come," has entered the common lexicon. It refers to the movie's plot, in which an Iowa farmer, Ray Kinsella, builds a baseball diamond in his cornfield to summon the late Shoeless Joe Jackson of the infamous 1919 Chicago White Sox (the team that threw the World Series), who comes to play some ball.

DID YOU KNOW?

After the movie was completed, test audiences apparently didn't like the title *Shoeless Joe* because it sounded too much like a movie about a homeless person. Universal changed the title to *Field of Dreams*. Kinsella wasn't upset about the change, though; *Shoeless Joe* was the name his publishers had given his story after vetoing the original title, *Dream Field*.

Cyberscribe

Few books have influenced pop culture quite as heavily as Vancouver-based science-fiction author William Gibson's 1984 debut novel *Neuromancer*. In it Gibson coined the term "cyberspace" and visualized a worldwide communications net 11 years before the Internet burst into public awareness. *Neuromancer* won all three major science-fiction awards—the Hugo, Nebula and Philip K. Dick—upon its release and has since sold more than 6.5 million copies worldwide. He also wrote two sequels—*Count Zero* (1986) and *Mona Lisa Overdrive* (1988)—and together the trilogy is considered the definitive work of the "cyberpunk" sci-fi subgenre.

DID YOU KNOW?

For many years, Gibson refused to get an Internet connection, saying the last thing he wanted after a day staring at his word processor was to carry on using the computer.

X Marks the Lot

The demographic-defining *Generation X: Tales for an Accelerated Culture* was the first book by West Vancouver native Douglas Coupland and made him the reluctant spokesperson for his generation. Despite being rejected by nearly 30 different publishers, his 1991 novel about a group of under-employed, over-educated 20-somethings hiding from the world in the Palm Springs desert has become part of the pop culture zeitgeist and is a book read by people who don't normally read books. It voices the angst-ridden concerns of a group negotiating an uncertain future of low-paid, temporary "McJobs" and was seized upon by ad agencies, trend analysts and film producers eager to win the hearts, minds and wallets of the so-called slacker generation.

While the term "Generation X" has become shorthand for all post-baby boom westerners born in the 1960s and early 1970s, Coupland was not the one who coined the term. Back in 1977, when the author was just 16, Generation X was a British punk rock band led by a young Billy Idol. The band stole the name from the title of a 1964 novel by Michael Jacobs about young Londoners in the swinging '60s. Mick Jagger was said to be a huge fan of Jacobs' book, and John Lennon tried to turn it into a musical.

ARCHITECTURAL ODDITIES

Straight and Narrow

Fan Tan Alley in Victoria's Chinatown is one of the narrowest streets in the world. Only 1.2 metres wide, it was once home to opium dens and Canada's first organized gambling houses. "Fan Tan" is the name of a popular Chinese game of chance.

Putting the Squeeze On

While the capital may have the narrowest street, Vancouver has the narrowest building, located at 8 Pender Street. It is only 1.5 metres wide, but 30 metres long. Sam Kee, a prominent businessman, built the two-storey structure in 1912 out of spite after the city appropriated his property to widen Pender Street, leaving him with only a thin strip of real estate. Below the sidewalk, a basement 3 metres wide extended the full length of the building. It was used as an underground bathhouse.

Floating Route

Completed in 1958, Kelowna's Floating Bridge over Lake Okanagan was the first of its kind in Canada. The bobbing bridge spans 650 metres, has three lanes and connects the city to Highway 97. It is currently being upgraded to five lanes, with completion expected in 2008.

Head in the Clouds

With an antenna height of 170 metres, Vancouver's Harbour Centre inches out the Alex Fraser Bridge (154 metres) and the Wall Centre (150 metres) as the highest structure in British Columbia.

DID YOU  KNOW?

Apart from the risk of earthquakes, the reason there are no substantially tall buildings in Vancouver is because laws exist to protect the view of the mountains. "View cones" were established to protect the view of the North Shore from key locations such as city hall and Queen Elizabeth Park.

Achiever Dam

At 242 metres, Mica Dam on the Columbia River near Revelstoke is the highest earth-filled dam in North America. Completed in 1973, its underground powerhouse was the largest in the world at the time and currently can generate up to 1805 megawatts.

Roger Dodger

The longest railway tunnel in the western hemisphere is the Mount Macdonald Tunnel, built under avalanche-prone Rogers Pass in the Selkirk Mountains. It is 14.6 kilometres long, cost $500 million in the mid-1980s and took five years to build.

People Who Live in Glass Houses

Overlooking Kootenay Lake in the town of Boswell is a house made out of half a million empty embalming fluid bottles. After travelling western Canada collecting the square-shaped bottles from colleagues, retired funeral director David Brown built the glass house in 1952 "to indulge a whim of a peculiar nature." It was meant to be the family home, but it garnered so much attention it became a tourist attraction instead.

Logging Cabin

The Cable Café, located in the town of Sayward on the east coast of Vancouver Island, is a restaurant made entirely of used logging cable. The walls contain 2500 metres of wire rope welded to an iron frame, and the building weighs almost 24 tonnes. Built by Glen Duncan, it opened as a restaurant in 1970. Forestry-related delicacies on the menu include Kusum Klimb burgers, Hoe Chuckers, Ringer Slingers and Whistle Punk sandwiches.

Park of the Beast

Park Place, the BC building with the most office space, not only shares the same name as a Monopoly property, but, located at 666 Burrard Street, also shares the number of the beast. Who do you think invented the rat race?

The Making of the Marine

One of the most recognizable buildings in the province is the 98-metre-tall art deco Marine Building at 355 Burrard Street, Vancouver's first "modern" skyscraper and the city's tallest building until 1939. Inspired by New York's Chrysler Building, it was designed to look like a rocky promontory rising from the sea. Back in the day, it used to be waterfront property before the harbour was filled in to make room for railway tracks and condominiums.

The Marine Building is filled with maritime touches. Brass bas-relief castings of starfish, crabs, seashells and sea horses surround the main entrance, while a 12-metre-high terra cotta arch above the door pays tribute to Captain George Vancouver, with his ship on the horizon framed by a rising sun. Awash in aqua greens and blues, the lobby is designed to resemble a huge, treasure-filled Mayan temple.

West Vancouver's Park Royal Shopping Centre has the distinction of being Canada's first shopping mall. It opened in September 1950 as an open-air mall and converted to an enclosed mall in 1962.

LIGHTS, CAMERA, ACTION

West End Girl

BC's first bona fide movie star was Peggy Yvonne Middleton, who grew up on Comox Street in Vancouver's West End in the 1920s. After moving to Hollywood in her teens, she changed her name to Yvonne De Carlo and was soon billed by publicists as "the most beautiful girl in the world." After a string of small roles in which she was little more than eye candy, the former dancer got her big break playing the lead in *Salome, Where She Danced* in 1945. Now with over 100 film credits under her belt, she is best known for playing Moses' wife in *The 10 Commandments* and monstrous housewife Lily Munster in the television series *The Munsters.* Her autobiography, *Yvonne*, was published in 1987.

DID YOU KNOW?

Yvonne De Carlo has been honoured with not one but two stars—one for movies and one for TV—on the Hollywood Walk of Fame.

Heavyweight Actor

The first Academy Award winner to make his mark in BC did so as a boxer. In 1909, Jack Johnson was the first black heavyweight champion. Unable to find boxers willing to fight him in the States, he took his title on the road and fought his first contender, Victor McLaglen, in Vancouver. McLaglen lasted six rounds with the champ. After retiring from the ring, he became an actor and won a best actor Oscar for his role in the 1935 film *The Informer.*

The Horror

Horror-film icon Boris Karloff first cut his teeth as an actor in BC. When the Englishman was touring the province in 1910 as a member of the Ray Brandon Players, a Kamloops theatre troupe, he stopped in Vancouver to make some better money and worked on the construction of the Pacific National Exhibition Centre. Not cut out to be a labourer, he decided instead to head south to Hollywood to try his luck there.

Victory Day

BC's first and most prolific Oscar winner was art director Richard Day. The Victoria native won his first gold statue for the 1935 film *The Dark Angel* and went on to win six more over his career for *Dodsworth, How Green Was My Valley, My Gal Sal, This Above All, A Streetcar Named Desire* and finally *On the Waterfront* in 1954. He received nominations for many more, including his final film in 1970, *Tora! Tora! Tora!*, which was about the Japanese attack on Pearl Harbor.

Luck of the Irish

The first actor from the province to be nominated for an Academy Award was John Ireland. Born in Vernon in 1914, Ireland was a nominee in the best supporting actor category for his role as reporter Jack Burden in the 1949 film *All the King's Men.* You might also remember him from such films as *Spartacus* and *Gunfight at the O.K. Corral.*

Blind Ambition

Animator Steve Bosustow was another BCer to find early success up on the big screen. The Victoria native's nearsighted 1949 creation Quincy Magoo was the first "human" cartoon character ever produced in Hollywood and went on to become one of the longest-running animated series ever. Voiced by Jim Backus, the cartoons were always a variation of the same joke—the cantankerous Mr. Magoo finds himself in sticky situations because of his failing eyesight—yet nonetheless managed to win two Oscars in the best short subjects category for *When Magoo Flew* (1954) and *Magoo's Puddle Jumper* (1955).

How Times Have Changed

A live-action version of Mr. Magoo filmed decades later in Vancouver starring Leslie Nielsen barely saw the light of day. As blind jokes are no longer considered a laughing matter, screenings were met with protests and reviews were brutal, causing the 1997 debacle to head straight to video.

An UnAmerican Canadian

Born in 1908, Edward Dmytryk is considered the first important film director to come from British Columbia. Although born in Grand Forks, he grew up in California and worked his way up the ranks from studio messenger boy to film editor to director. The son of Ukrainian immigrants, Dmytryk joined the Communist Party and made several politically charged films such as the anti-fascist *Hitler's Children* and *Crossfire*, one of the first Hollywood movies to tackle anti-Semitism, for which he was nominated for best director at the 1947 Academy Awards. Summoned by Senator Joe McCarthy to appear before the House Committee on Un-American Activities (HUAC), he was one of the famous Hollywood 10 who refused to testify and was sentenced to a year in prison for contempt of Congress. He was also blacklisted from making movies, along with dozens of other artists.

A few years later, struggling financially, he turned on his former comrades, revealing the names of other Communists to HUAC, and was allowed to return to his Hollywood career. Considered a traitor by many, he went on to direct 25 more films, including such notable flicks as *The Caine Mutiny*, *Walk on the Wild Side* and *The Carpetbaggers*.

Everyone Loved Raymond

Raymond Burr was a renowned actor whose commanding presence graced over 90 feature films, several television shows, more than 5000 radio plays and over 200 theatre productions. Born in New Westminster in 1917, he initially worked as a ranch hand, deputy sheriff and nightclub singer before joining the Navy during World War II. After he was shot in the stomach and sent home, he made his acting debut in the 1946 film *San Quentin.* Burr went on to star in such notable films as *A Cry in the Night, A Place in the Sun, Godzilla* and Alfred Hitchcock's classic *Rearview Mirror.* He is best remembered, however, for his long-running television roles as unbeatable attorney Perry Mason (1957–93) and paraplegic policeman Robert Ironside (1967–75).

The city of New Westminster has declared May 31 to be Raymond Burr Day in recognition of his achievements.

 The Raymond Burr Performing Arts Centre in New Westminster, a 238-seat theatre, opened in 2000 near a city block bearing the Burr family name. It is customary for every play performed there to have a photo of Burr included somewhere on the set.

Because it was considered career suicide in those days for a leading man to be openly gay, Burr claimed to have been married twice, but both his wives had died. He lived with his partner, Robert Benevides, for 35 years until Burr's death from kidney cancer in 1993. Burr's body is buried in New Westminster's Fraser Cemetery.

Flynn Done In

The biggest movie star to end his career in BC is unquestionably Errol Flynn. In October 1959, the flamboyant 50-year-old former matinee idol came to town to sell his luxury yacht, *Zaca*, to local businessman George Caldough. Arriving with a teenaged girl in tow, Flynn stayed at the swanky Hotel Georgia, and the couple spent a wild week making the rounds of all the downtown nightclubs. As they were being taken to the airport for their flight home to Hollywood, the actor complained of back pains, so Caldough drove them instead to the house of his friend Dr. Grant Gould (the uncle of famed pianist Glenn Gould) in the West End. Flynn went for a brief nap in the doctor's bedroom with the famous last words "I shall return." He didn't.

Wild West Vancouver

The first film shot in BC to be nominated for an Oscar was Robert Altman's 1972 film *McCabe & Mrs. Miller*. The legendary Julie Christie was nominated for best actress playing the madam of a bordello opposite Warren Beatty in this gritty western shot in West Van's Cyprus Park.

The Old Man and the CPR

The Grey Fox was considered a landmark film when it was
released in 1982 and continues to be lauded even today. The
film helped kick-start the BC film industry and gave some much-
needed credibility to Canadian-made movies by winning 10
Genie awards. It was directed by Maple Ridge's Philip Borsos,
a former protégé of Francis Ford Coppola, and starred the late
character actor and stuntman Richard Farnsworth as Bill Miner,
otherwise known as the "gentleman bandit."

The film was not only shot in various locations in the province,
but was also based on a true BC story.

On a foggy fall evening near Mission in 1904, Bill Miner
and two accomplices robbed the Canadian Pacific Railway's
Transcontinental Express. Their take was $7000 in cash and
$300,000 in bonds and securities (worth more than $5 million
in today's dollars). Miner was formerly a specialist in robbing
stagecoaches. This was his first successful train holdup and
Canada's first train robbery.

Miner, 56, had over four decades of holdups to his name. He is
credited with coining the phrase "Hands up" and was famous for
always apologizing to his victims for the inconvenience. As many
westerners despised the all-powerful CPR, and because he had
a reputation for never firing his gun, Miner became something
of a local folk hero.

A Gentlemen and His Collar

But he wasn't quite as lucky on his next try. On May 16, 1906, he and his gang targeted a Canadian Pacific train at Ducks, just east of Kamloops. He made the mistake of going after the baggage car instead of the express car and didn't notice his mistake until he'd already ordered the engineer to drive away. Although the train had been carrying $70,000 in cash and bullion, the gang's entire take from the heist was a mere $15 and some liver pills.

Less than a week later, the desperadoes were captured near Douglas Lake. All three were tried and convicted in a courtroom at Kamloops, and Miner was sentenced to life imprisonment.

The Fake Escape

Unless the CPR could recover the $300,000 Miner had stashed, it would have to reimburse the government for the stolen funds, so the company sent a private detective to visit Miner in jail, promising he'd be allowed to "escape" if he would lead them to the money. Three months later he did just that, and the federal government was repaid, though it was none too happy (Prime Minister Wilfrid Laurier in particular) about the price paid to get it back. Although the Mounties tried to recapture their man, the Grey Fox had already fled the country to continue his career in the south.

Sister Act

Victoria's Meg Tilly received an Oscar nomination for best supporting actress in 1985 for her role as a pregnant nun in the film *Agnes of God*. Not to be outdone, her big sister Jennifer was nominated in the same category a decade later for her performance as an untalented actress in the Woody Allen comedy *Bullets Over Broadway*. Both actresses have also shot feature films in their home province: Meg with *Leaving Normal* (1992), and Jennifer with *Deluxe Combo Platter* (2003), *Man With A Gun* (1995) and *Double Cross* (1994).

Victimized in Vancouver

The first movie shot in BC to win an Academy Award was *The Accused.* Jodie Foster won the second Oscar of her career playing the survivor of a gang rape in the 1988 film based on a true story. Along with multiple shots of the UBC campus, the Vancouver Art Gallery stands in for the legal drama's courthouse, and the scene of the crime, the Tidewaters Pub in Delta, remains open for business to this day.

DID YOU KNOW?

While *The Accused* remains the only Oscar winner filmed in BC, Cairo-born and Victoria-raised director Atom Egoyan's equally grim *The Sweet Hereafter* (shot in and around the Merritt and Spences Bridge region) was nominated in 1998 in both the best director and best writing categories.

Vancouver's Lions Gate Films is currently the biggest independent film distributor in North America. Originally founded by director Robert Altman (*Gosford Park, M.A.S.H.*) in 1970, it is named for the famous bridge near Stanley Park. Among the studio's early successes were *The Late Show, Images* and *A Wedding.* Altman sold the company in 1981.

Frank Giustra, a local banker/financier hoping to cash in on Vancouver's booming new film biz, launched the current version in 1997. Its first big success came as distributor of the gruesome film *American Psycho,* which led to the company finding a niche producing and/or distributing films deemed too hot to handle by mainstream American studios.

Other notable films produced by Lions Gate Films that have received Oscar nods over the years include:

Affliction (1998)
Best supporting actor (winner)—James Coburn
Best actor (nominated)—Nick Nolte

Gods and Monsters (1998)
Best actor (nominated)—Ian McKellen

Monster's Ball (2001)
Best actress (winner)—Halle Berry

Hotel Rwanda (2004)
Best actor (nominated)—Don Cheadle
Best actress (nominated)—Sophie Okonedo

Bowling for Columbine (2002)
Best documentary (winner)—Michael Moore

Crash (2005)
Best picture (winner)—Paul Haggis
Best screenplay (winner)—Paul Haggis, Robert Moresco
Best editing (winner)—Hughes Winborne
Best supporting actor (nominated)—Matt Dillon
Best director (nominated)—Paul Haggis

DID YOU  KNOW?

Lions Gate isn't the only Oscar-winning studio in BC. Infinity Media saw its 2005 production *Capote* nominated in five different categories, with Philip Seymour Hoffman winning for best actor.

BC Filmmakers Made Good

My American Cousin (1985)
Set in the Okanagan region during the 1950s, Sandy Wilson's coming-of-age tale won six Genie awards and the Critics' Award at the Toronto International Film Festival.

The Lotus Eaters (1993)
Sheila McCarthy won a Genie for best actress, playing a radical rural high school teacher during the 1960s in this film by Paul Shapiro. Peggy Thompson's screenplay earned her a Genie as well, and the film was voted the most popular Canadian film at the Vancouver International Film Festival.

Double Happiness (1994)
Sandra Oh won a best actress Genie for her role in Mina Shum's interracial romantic comedy, voted best Canadian feature at the Toronto International Film Festival.

Kissed (1996)
Lynne Stopkewich's controversial film about a young woman who "sees" dead people won the best Canadian feature title at the Toronto International Film Festival, and Molly Parker won a best actress Genie for playing the necrophiliac mortuary worker.

Suspicious River (2000)
Lynne Stopkewich and Molly Parker's next collaboration, about a motel receptionist who sells her body to guests in more ways than one, won Leo awards for best cinematography, best feature and best actor (Callum Keith Rennie).

The Corporation (2003)
Based on a book by UBC law professor Joel Bakan, this documentary by Jennifer Abbott and Mark Achbar about the inherently unethical nature of public corporations won eight international audience choice awards, including one from the Sundance Film Festival.

Last Wedding (2001)
Bruce Sweeney's pitch-black romantic comedy was named best Canadian feature at the Toronto International Film Festival, while Vincent Gale and Molly Parker earned Genies for best supporting actor and actress.

Scared Sacred (2004)
Velcrow Ripper's film about searching for hope in some the world's saddest places (Ground Zero, Hiroshima, Chernobyl) earned a Genie award for best documentary and both a special jury citation and best Canadian feature title at the Toronto International Film Festival.

Eve and the Fire Horse (2005)
Filmed in Vancouver's Chinatown, Julia Kwan's debut feature about two Chinese Canadian sisters with big imaginations was awarded a special Jury prize at the Sundance Film Festival.

A to Z of Some Films Made in BC

Alive (1993)

Best in Show (2000)

Clan of the Cave Bear (1986)

Double Jeopardy (1999)

Emile (2003)

First Blood (1982)

Ghost Ship (2002)

Happy Gilmore (1996)

Insomnia (2002)

Josie & the Pussycats (2001)

Kiss the Girls (1997)

Legends of the Fall (1994)

Miracle (2004)

Needful Things (1993)

On The Corner (2003)

The Pledge (2001)

Quarantine (1989)

Roxanne (1987)

Scary Movie (2000)

The Thing (1982)

An Unfinished Life (2005)

Van Wilder (2002)

Wrongfully Accused (1998)

X-Men 2 and 3 (2003, 2006)

Year of the Dragon (1985)

Zacharia Farted (1998)

BC ON THE BOOB TUBE

Making Waves

The first person in the world to earn a paycheque by being on TV was born in Nelson in 1910. Joan Miller was originally a stage actress who moved to England when she was unable to find work at home. She worked in radio and wrote a sketch for herself in which she played a switchboard operator. It was later adapted by the BBC for *Picture Page*, the world's first television program, which was broadcast on November 2, 1936. Miller played the "Picture Page Girl," earning £12 a week, until the show was cancelled after Germany went and ruined things for everyone. She is also said to be the first performer broadcast across the Atlantic after someone in Long Island reported picking up a transmission of the show.

Going For Brogue

The late actor James Doohan, best known for his long-running role as engineer Montgomery "Scotty" Scott of the *Star Trek* franchise, was born in Vancouver in 1920. At the outbreak of World War II, 19-year-old Doohan joined the Royal Canadian Artillery and was sent to England for what became years of training in beach assault tactics. He first saw combat during the invasion of Normandy on D-Day. After making two confirmed kills, he was hit by six German bullets: four in his leg, one in the chest, and one through his middle right finger, a disfigurement he always took care to hide when he became an actor.

Fittingly, following his death from pneumonia in 2005, he boldly went where no man has gone before when his cremated remains were released into orbit from a rocket blasted from California's Vandenberg Air Force Base.

Doohan's natural ability with foreign accents is what earned him the role of Scotty. When auditioning for Gene Rodenberry, he tried a variety before settling on a Scottish brogue, saying, "If you're going to have an engineer, you'd better make him Scottish." When *Star Trek: The Animated Series* was produced in the early 1970s, he provided a wide variety of voices for different characters. He also came up with the early examples of Vulcan and Klingon dialogue.

Play It Again, Scotty

Although Doohan became inextricably linked with the line "Beam me up, Scotty," the actual phrase was never uttered in either the series or movies. The closest anyone came was in *Star Trek IV: The Voyage Home*, when Captain Kirk said, "Scotty, beam me up."

The Horse Listener

Former CBC radio host Alan Young was one of the next people from the province to hit the big time on the tube. Born in Scotland but raised in Vancouver, Young found fame playing architect Wilbur Pope opposite the talking horse known as Mr. Ed on the program of the same name. *Mr. Ed* won a Golden Globe award for best TV show in 1963, and though the show ceased production three years later, reruns are still broadcast on many channels around the world. Young has since made a number of TV and film appearances but is known primarily for his voice work in cartoons, especially as Donald Duck's Uncle Scrooge.

On the Waterfront

The Beachcombers (1972–91)
With 387 episodes broadcast over 19 years, this family-friendly show is the longest-running TV series in Canadian history. Filmed in and around the picturesque town of Gibsons on the Sunshine Coast near Vancouver, the show starred Bruno Gerussi as professional log salvager Nick Adonidas and Robert Clothier as his nemesis, Relic. The series sold to over 60 countries around the world from Abu Dhabi to Australia, and over 10,000 tourists have since come to the area to see where it was filmed. *The Beachcombers* was cancelled because of CBC budget cuts rather than poor ratings. Despite the fact Gerussi and Clothier are now both dead, CBC brass have since tried to resurrect the show with *The New Beachcombers* in 2002 and *A Beachcomber's Christmas*, with little success.

DID YOU KNOW?

The show's hangout, "Molly's Reach," still survives today and remains a popular tourist attraction.

Goodfella

Wiseguy (1987–90)
This multiple-Emmy-nominated series starred Ken Wahl as Vinnie Terranova, a government agent so deep undercover even his own mother thought he was a bad guy. Boob-tube guru Stephen J. Cannell's crime drama was one of the first to show empathy for characters on both sides of the law and to have an ongoing narrative instead of the usual tidy ending for each episode. The show helped launch the career of Kevin Spacey and earned Wahl a Golden Globe for best actor.

Veneration X

The X-Files (1993–2002)

This creepy Fox series about the adventures of Mulder and Scully, two improbably attractive FBI agents investigating vast government conspiracies and things that go bump in the night, was one of the biggest shows in television history. The show helped put Vancouver on the map as a movie-making destination, won dozens of awards (including several Emmys and Golden Globes) and lives on in perpetual syndication. The show was cancelled in its ninth season after production moved to California.

DID YOU  KNOW?

The famous echoing chord from the theme music was a fluke. Composer Mark Snow accidentally rested his elbow on his keyboard while the echo function was on. He liked the resulting sound so much, he wrote the theme around it.

Aliens at the Gate

Stargate SG-1 (1997–)
With its recently announced upcoming 10th season, this Emmy-nominated series about a special forces unit that boldly goes where no one has gone before after discovering interplanetary portals allowing instantaneous travel across the universe has overtaken *The X-Files* as TV's longest-running science-fiction series. It is also the only television show in history endorsed and supported by the Pentagon. Based on a 1994 film starring James Spader and Vancouver resident Kurt Russell, in 2002, *SG-1* spawned a spinoff of its own, *Stargate Atlantis*, which is also shot in BC. The show has won four Saturn awards, two Geminis and nine Leo awards during its run.

DID YOU  KNOW?

The prop that looks like a wand, which is used to control the Tok'ra memory recall device, is actually an electric nose-hair trimmer.

The Eh Team

Cold Squad (1998–2005)
This gritty CTV drama about Vancouver coppers was so named not because of the chilly Canadian climate, but because the squad was in charge of solving unsolved cases that had been in the "cold" file for many years. Along with a slew of other nominations, it won seven Gemini awards and a best actress Leo for Alisen Down.

DID YOU  **KNOW?**

In 2003, American producers came out with the notably similar *Cold Case,* leading to legal action from the producers of *Cold Squad.* CTV, however, didn't seem to mind and happily carried both shows.

Campbell's Group

Da Vinci's Inquest (1998–2005)
Da Vinci's City Hall (2005–06)

Among the highest-rated and most-lauded TV shows in Canadian history, these CBC dramas were like a fictional mirror of the city of Vancouver. The lead character, Dominic Da Vinci (Nicholas Campbell), was based on Larry Campbell, a former Mountie who became the city's chief coroner and later the mayor. Campbell served as a technical advisor in the show's early days and arguably was voted into office largely because of Vancouverites' fondness for Da Vinci. Many of the issues explored on the show—the Downtown Eastside's missing women, safe-injection sites, police brutality and gay-bashing in Stanley Park—were based on actual events.

Mad Max

Dark Angel (2000–02)

This Fox series starred Jessica Alba as Max Guevara, a genetically enhanced überbabe who escaped from a secret government institution (actually Coquitlam's Riverview Hospital) and became a courier in a post-apocalyptic world. James Cameron's award-winning cyberpunk series was terminated after only two seasons, mainly because, in the wake of 9/11, viewers no longer had much of an appetite for a show set in a world destroyed by terrorists.

Alba later returned to Vancouver to play *Fantastic Four* member Sue Storm, yet another super-powered heroine.

Future Tense

Andromeda (2000–05)
This *Buck Rogers* rip-off starred Kevin Sorbo as a spaceship captain who found himself beamed centuries into the future and faced with the Herculean task of saving the universe. Particularly acclaimed for its special effects and makeup, the awards won by *Star Trek* creator Gene Rodenberry's posthumous baby include a Leo for best direction, several Geminis and gold plaques from the Chicago International Film Festival.

Teen of Steel

Smallville (2001–)
This Emmy-winning Warner Brothers series follows the teenage adventures of Clark Kent (Tom Welling) before he became Superman. The Surrey suburb of Cloverdale stands in for the superhero's boyhood home, while nearby Vancouver doubles as Metropolis.

DID YOU KNOW?

Lex Luthor's mansion is actually Hatley Castle of Victoria's Royal Roads University, an address he shares with Professor Xavier's School for Gifted Mutants from the *X-Men* film franchise. Annette O'Toole, who plays Ma Kent, also appeared in 1983's *Superman III* as Lana Lang.

Space Truckin'

Battlestar Galactica (2003–)

This revival of the 1970s cult show was originally only intended to be a miniseries, but it was so popular, the Sci-Fi Channel ordered more episodes and turned it into a series. The premise is that a colony of humans in a galaxy far, far away, after nearly being wiped out by cybernetic Cylons, travel in a convoy through space in search of the mythical planet Earth. Largely shot inside a studio, the show also makes good use of the distinctive architecture of the Vancouver Public Library and Simon Fraser University campus. The surprise hit series won a Hugo award—science fiction's answer to the Stanley Cup—in 2005 and received an Emmy nomination for its special effects the same year.

DID YOU  **KNOW?**

The shuttle dock onboard the *Colonial One*—with lane markers left visible—is clearly the car deck of a BC ferry.

BC TV R.I.P

Danger Bay (1984–89)

MacGyver (1985–92)

Stingray (1986–87)

21 Jump Street (1987–91)

Booker (1989–90)

Bordertown (1989–94)

Neon Rider (1990–95)

The Commish (1991–95)

The Highlander (1992–98)

Madison (1993–97)

Outer Limits (1995–2002)

Millennium (1996–99)

Breaker High (1997–98)

Dead Man's Gun (1997–99)

Harsh Realm (1999–2000)

Edgemont (2000–05)

The Chris Isaak Show (2001–04)

The Twilight Zone (2002–03)

Dead Like Me (2003–04)

EVEN MORE BC TRIVIA

Rabble's Babble

While most Canadians now associate the word "chinook" with a welcome winter warm snap east of the Rockies, once upon a time it was a language shared by as many as 250,000 people from all over the world. Because so many different languages evolved among the various First Nations communities scattered throughout the Pacific Northwest, Chinook Jargon became a common tongue used to communicate between groups. The pidgin trade language was adopted and expanded by newcomers to the area—whether European, Asian, Aboriginal or miscellaneous—and soon became the lingua franca throughout the region. If a Spaniard wanted to rent a room from a Chinese, a "Bostoner" (American) wanted to swap goods with a Cree, or a Frenchman needed directions from a British *Kinchotsh* (for "King George"), they'd probably speak in Chinook.

While Chinook began to decline after BC joined Confederation, some of the words still remain in popular use. "Skookum" is common BC slang for something big, strong, or way cool, while "muckamuck" refers to some sort of bigshot.

Kid Rock

Most male radio deejays wait until after their voices crack before they hit the airwaves. Not so with Cody Morton, who entered the history books by becoming the world's youngest disc jockey at the age of 10 with his "Bust a Groove" show on Tofino's CHOO FM. By 14 he had moved up on the dial to Port Alberni's CJAV 1240 with a show specializing in emo and indie rock. He remains there today.

Bowser's Boozehound

Health codes weren't quite as restrictive back in the 1930s. At the Bowser Hotel near Qualicum Beach on the east coast of Vancouver Island, a dog named Mike used to serve beer to patrons, collect their cash and return with their change...and accept scratches on the head as a tip.

Tomb Trader

Peter Verigin, leader of a breakaway Russian Christian sect, known as the Doukhobors, that came to Canada to escape persecution at home, lies beneath the biggest tombstone in BC. Surrounded by barbed wire, the 10-metre-high tomb is located on a rocky ledge above the Kootenay River and is the occupant's second final resting place after his original white marble tomb was mysteriously blown up. It was the second explosion for "Peter the Lordly." Verigin died in 1924 after a train he was travelling in exploded; an event most believe was an assassination by a splinter Doukhobor sect—likely the same culprits who later desecrated his grave.

Mandrake's Roots

Mandrake the Magician was born in New Westminster in 1911. An accomplished conjurer, illusionist, mentalist, manipulator, ventriloquist and fire-eater, the top-hatted, pencil-mustachioed performer became one of the most famous magicians in the world and, along with his partner and wife Velvet, was the first to stage magic shows in nightclub settings, inviting audience participation.

DID YOU  KNOW?

Mandrake the Magician was the first super-powered, costumed crime fighter in comics, battling the forces of evil several years before Superman first got into the act. Inspired by the tuxedoed magician, Lee Falk created the long-running cartoon character in 1934.

Sea to Shining Sea

When Thomas Wilby and Jack Haney arrived in Port Alberni in October 1912, they became the first people to drive all the way across Canada. There was no national highway back then, and very few good provincial roads. Wilby and Haney left Halifax behind the wheel of a brand new REO, a car built by Ransom E. Olds—whose initials gave the car its name. (Later, Olds used his name again when he launched the Oldsmobile.) The journey took 49 days.

High Snorer

The dubious distinction of being the loudest snorer in the world once belonged to Mark Hebbard of Richmond. Testers from UBC recorded his nocturnal emissions at 90 decibels—10 higher than the city's noise bylaw allows and roughly as loud as a police siren—before he finally had corrective surgery.

Battle Star

The first spot in western Canada where Native culture was officially commemorated can be found just east of the town of Terrace. Located on the Kitwanga River and overlooking ancient trails leading to the Skeena, Nass and Stikine rivers, the Kitwanga Fort National Historic Site memorializes a Native stronghold called Ta'awdzep, or Battle Hill, which burned to the ground in the early 19th century as the Gitwangak First Nation defended its trades route from encroaching tribes.

According to legend, a badass warrior named Nekt was in charge of the fort. His battle dress was said to be a grizzly bear skin lined with slate, and he wielded a magical truncheon called Strike-Only-Once. In order to defend the hilltop, he secured huge logs to the fort's fence and released them to roll down and crush the enemy.

HECK OF A BROWNIE

One of the great unsolved mysteries is whether BC's famous Nanaimo bars were actually invented in, or by someone from, the eastern Vancouver Island community of the same name. Nobody knows for sure the source of the recipe or its name, or even where the first Nanaimo bar appeared.

The Truth Is Out There

A cookbook published by Canadian candy merchants Laura Secord claims that the Nanaimo bar was invented by a "well-known" food company but neglects to name names, and no company has ever officially claimed the tasty treat as its own. Others claim the recipe first appeared in a Nanaimo hospital cookbook published in the 1950s, but no copies of the book can be found, if in fact it ever existed. Some theorists maintain the dessert first made its debut as a "Chocolate Fridge Cake" in a 1936 issue of the *Vancouver Sun*, yet all efforts by the newspaper's archivists to confirm this have failed. Another theory has Dutch settlers bringing the recipe with them in the early 1900s.

Staking a Claim

Whatever the bar's origins, Nanaimo's Chamber of Commerce has cemented the city's claim to fame by producing the following official recipe, which is released only with imperial measures:

BOTTOM LAYER
½ cup unsalted butter
¼ cup sugar
5 Tbsp cocoa
1 beaten egg
1¾ cup graham crumbs
½ cup finely chopped almonds
1 cup coconut

Melt the first three ingredients in a pot. Add the egg and stir to thicken. Remove from heat. Stir in remaining ingredients and press firmly into an ungreased 8" x 8" pan.

MIDDLE LAYER
½ cup unsalted butter
2 Tbsp cream
2 Tbsp vanilla custard powder
2 cups icing sugar

Cream ingredients together and beat until light. Spread over bottom layer.

TOP LAYER
4 squares semi-sweet chocolate
2 Tbsp unsalted butter

Melt ingredients over low heat. Cool. When cool, pour over middle layer and chill in refrigerator. Enjoy!

MADE IN BC

Ten world-famous products that saw the light of day in British Columbia.

MUTANT DNA

University of British Columbia researcher Michael Smith was awarded the 1993 Nobel Prize in Chemistry for his work on site-based mutagenics, a newfangled technique for purposefully changing the DNA sequence of any gene. His work laid the foundations for today's biotechnology breakthroughs and led to a better understanding of how to treat cancers and viruses. He also donated his entire half-million-dollar prize to some local charities—Science World in particular.

HELI-SKIING

Hans Gmoser, an Austrian-born mountain guide, was the first person to come up with the bright idea of using helicopters to access remote mountaintop powder. In 1965, after teaming up with pilot Jim Davies and setting up shop in an abandoned lumber camp at the base of the Bugaboos, he began offering commercial tours on the pristine peaks of the Columbia Valley in eastern BC. Said to be more addictive than cocaine and twice as expensive, the pricey pursuit has become a major component of BC's tourism industry, and imitators have since popped up on every continent.

THE NEWTSUIT

Wearing a Newtsuit is like slipping into your very own personal submarine. Created by Phil Nuytten of North Vancouver, the aquatic suit of armour allows divers to descend to depths of 700 metres, where, in spite of the enormous surrounding pressure, its unique joint design allows the operator to pick things up and move around with 75 percent of the dexterity of a diver at normal depths. The suit also maintains an interior pressure equal to the pressure at sea level, so the operator doesn't need to go through lengthy decompression on the way back up.

Pictionary

Rob Angel was working in Vancouver as a waiter back in 1986 when he came up with the idea for a board game that would mix charades with doodling—instead of acting out clues, players would guess the identities of words by drawing clues for each other. Although Angel initially had to go door-to-door in an attempt to get people interested in what he named Pictionary, it has since gone on to become a worldwide phenomenon, generating nearly $1 billion in total retail sales over the past two decades.

Buy Nothing Day

This international event, in which people participate simply by not participating, is the brainchild of Vancouver-based Adbusters Media Foundation. The idea behind the annual affair is to draw attention to the wasteful consumption habits of the western world and to demonstrate economic clout over the global economy by refusing to spend a single red cent over a 24-hour period. Since the early 1990s, Buy Nothing Day has been held in North America on the fourth Friday of November (the day after American Thanksgiving and traditionally one of the busiest shopping days of the year)—and on the last Saturday of November in the rest of the world.

Marsh Pegs

Far fewer hockey players have to head to the hospital these days thanks to the brainchild of Kitimat rink rat Fred Marsh. Concerned by the injuries local players were receiving after crashing into the metal goal posts, he created a more flexible type of rod to anchor the posts to the ice that would allow the net to move upon impact but not enough to be dislodged through regular play. The NHL adopted his assist to the game in 1991.

BC Bud

British Columbia is currently the cannabis capital of the world.
In fact, BC Bud is so popular it's unofficially rated as the
province's number one export and top industry, even ahead of
logging and fishing. Experts at the Organized Crime Agency
estimate the province has around 15,000 to 25,000 marijuana
grow operations employing between 90,000 and 150,000 people,
and the crop's annual wholesale value is around $4 billion. It's
estimated that about 75 percent of it goes directly to the insatiable
American market, where penalties for cultivation can mean life in
prison rather than just a slap on the wrist.

Generation II Knee Brace

One can only guess how many thousands of people have been
able to continue taking part in the activities they love thanks
to the work of Richmond orthotist Geordie Taylor. Built to
match the natural movements of the knee, his joint creation
has become the bestselling knee brace in the world and is worn
by such star athletes as Steve Yzerman, Hermann Maier and
Shaquille O'Neal.

THE LIGHT PIPE

A light bulb went on over the head of UBC physics student Lorne Whitehead after he became fed up with the poor quality of fluorescent lighting in the university's basement lab. He created a new source of lighting using hollow rectangular tubes covered with small angulated prisms. When a light source is put at one end of the tube, the light is evenly reflected and transmitted down the tube's entire length.

The Light Pipe has a slew of practical applications. They make it easy to achieve special effects with colour filters, evidenced by the 15-metre-high arches that marked the monorail at Expo 86. They are also used to light hazardous areas, where the heat from a normal light bulb or potential sparks could cause problems, and to light cold storage areas, where servicing a light can be difficult. They are also often used to highlight the features of such landmarks as New York's IBM Building, London's Millennium Bridge and the Neues Kranzler Building in Berlin.

HYDROGEN FUEL CELLS

The planet's first fuel-cell-powered, zero-emission vehicle was unveiled in 1993 by Burnaby's Ballard Power Systems. The technology used is the invention of Dr. Geoffrey Ballard, named a "Hero of the Planet" by *Time* magazine in 1999, and not to be confused with the Doctor Ballard of dog-food fame. Ballard hopes to someday create a feasible alternative to the internal combustion engine, using fuel cells that turn methanol into hydrogen, which means water vapour would come out the exhaust pipe instead of poison. The company's focus so far has been on building public transit buses, but if things go according to plan, fuel-cell cars could be a commercial reality by 2012. The company has been commissioned to service 27 Mercedes-Benz Citaro fuel-cell buses that will operate on European roads as part of the Clean Urban Transport for Europe project.

INITIAL REPORT

BC has long been the common shorthand for British Columbia. However, the province is but one of many BCs—there are over a dozen others in many different walks of life.

BEFORE CHRIST

The most commonly known BC is, of course, the acronym used to refer to time before the year Jesus was born. This time period is now often rendered as the more politically correct BCE, meaning either "before the Common Era" or "before the Christian Era." To the truly PC, BC can also refer to the time "before Columbus" stumbled across North America in 1492.

BEFORE COMPUTERS

While the pre-computer era was only half a century ago, it can sometimes seem as distant as the time of Christ. This other BC era harkens back to the days when a hard drive meant a long road trip, an application was for finding a job, a keyboard was part of a piano and memory was something you lost over time.

BOSTON COLLEGE

Also known as BC or The Heights, this university in Chestnut Hill, Massachusetts, is one of the oldest Jesuit schools in America. Interestingly, before joining the BC Lions, Canadian football hero Doug Flutie was the quarterback for the BC Eagles from 1981 to 1984. Flutie won the Heisman Trophy with them in his senior year after connecting with Gerard Phelan in one of college football's best-known plays—a game-winning Hail Mary pass tossed from his own 37-yard line into the Miami Hurricanes' end zone in the dying seconds.

Ballistic Coefficient

To gun owners, BC refers to a bullet's ballistic coefficient, the measure of air drag calculated by a ratio of its density to its coefficient of form. In other words, a bullet's mass is divided by the diameter squared that it presents to the airflow. A bullet with a high BC will go farther than one with a low BC.

Baja California

British Columbia shares an abbreviation with Mexico's northernmost state, which also managed to score the letters BC as its postal code. British Columbia's association with Baja may have more significant roots in time and space according to the contentious geological "Baja British Columbia" theory. According to some geoscientists, large parts of western British Columbia moved northward from latitudes that correspond to those of Baja California about 60 to 100 million years ago.

Bechuanaland

BC used to be NATO's two-letter country code for this landlocked southern African nation before its citizens kicked the British out in 1966 and changed the name to Botswana.

B.C. by Johnny Hart

Debuting in February 1958, this comic strip about prehistoric cavemen and anthropomorphic animals from different geologic eras is one of the longest-running daily newspaper strips in history. Hart hails from the town of Endicott in Broome County, New York, and clearly is the town's favourite son. The county parks department features a statue of his green dinosaur; his distinctive drawing of a caveman riding a wheel is plastered on every BC Transit bus; and a caveman on skates is the logo for Broome County's hockey team, the BC Icemen. A PGA Tour event, the BC Open, has been held annually since 1971 and also uses one of Hart's characters as its logo.

BASIC CALCULATOR

To the mathematically inclined, bc refers to the Unix programming code used in scripting. Similar to the C programming language, there are currently two main dialects: the precise POSIX bc and its direct, wider-ranging descendant GNU bc.

BLISS BIBLIOGRAPHIC CLASSIFICATION

Not nearly as popular as the Dewey Decimal system, the Bliss bibliographic classification (BC for short) is a cataloguing system that was created by librarian Henry Bliss in 1940. Although devised in the United States, it was more commonly adopted in the United Kingdom. A revised edition of this system (BC2) was developed in 1977.

BECAUSE

To text messagers too busy to include the letters *e, a, u* and *s,* the word "because" is often shortened to bc.

BOOKCROSSING

This is the name given to the practice of leaving a book in a public place to be picked up and read by others. Called "BCing" for short, it involves "releasing into the wild" books that have been registered at BookCrossing.com so when someone finds them, they can visit the site and track the journey the book took before reaching them. The idea came from the practice of placing electronic tags on animals and following their movements.

Committed Burst size

The maximum committed amount of data you can offer to any given computer network is defined as Bc. In other words, Bc is a measure of the number of bits for which a network can guarantee message delivery under normal Internet congestion conditions.

Brunswick Corporation

BC is the stock symbol for the Brunswick Corporation, a Fortune 500 consumer sporting goods manufacturer known primarily for its billiard tables and bowling balls.

Buoyancy Compensator

To a scuba diver, BC (or BCD for buoyancy control device) is a buoyancy compensator, a piece of equipment that controls flotation and the diver's ability to ascend or descend.

Backward-Compatible

In computer technology, something is said to have BC, or backward compatibility, when there is an interface allowing successful exchanges between components and products that were each developed separately. Usually shortened to "compatible," it is the term for new programs that still work with old hardware.

B.C. XBox

B.C. is a third-person adventure video game released by Microsoft in 2005. Set in a prehistoric world, the game challenges players to take control of a tribe of humans who face predators, natural disasters and the search for food while battling a simian race vying for evolutionary supremacy.

HOW TO SPEAK LIKE A BRITISH COLUMBIAN

2010: Shorthand term for a two-week international sporting event hosted by Vancouver and Whistler in the winter of 2010. Also a common explanation for all manner of unexpected economic changes, e.g., "How come your prices went up?" "2010."

Abby: Abbotsford

Aircare: An emission inspection all vehicles in the Greater Vancouver area must pass in order to be licensed. Often circumvented by owners of beaters who run a tank of high-octane gas through the engine beforehand

All Good: An expression denoting well-being. Generally a reassurance rather than a statement, e.g., "What's it like having to move back in with your parents?" "It's all good."

Back East: Anywhere in Canada on the other side of the Rocky Mountains

The Big Smoke: Vancouver. Predating the city's current infamy as a marijuana mecca, the nickname was coined in the mid 19th century either because of the city's many mills or because "smoke" also referred to clouds and fog in Chinook jargon. The fact downtown Vancouver burned to the ground in 1886 probably helped the name stick as well

Billy's Puddle: Williams Lake. Also known as Willy's Puddle or simply The Lake

Canucklehead: A fan of the Vancouver Canucks hockey team

Cave-On-Foods: Save-On-Foods. This nickname for the chain of grocery stores became popular after a rooftop parking lot collapsed on the Station Square Mall outlet in Richmond.

The Charlottes: The Queen Charlotte Islands, aka Haida Gwaii

Chuck: A Chinook word for a substantial body of water. A salt chuck refers specifically to seawater, e.g., "You've got to cross a big salt chuck to reach the Charlottes."

Coqui-killya: An epithet for the treacherous Coquihalla Highway linking the Vancouver area to the Okanagan

The Cove: The North Vancouver community of Deep Cove, not to be confused with the Saanich Peninsula community of Deep Cove

The Couv: Vancouver

Ditchmond: They say that for every kilometre of road in Richmond, there are two kilometres of ditches. Because the city lies mostly below sea level, a vast drainage system of ditches and culverts has been constructed to prevent it from being washed away by the tides or the Fraser River.

The Dole: Welfare. See "Pogey."

The Drive: The East Vancouver countercultural district located around Commercial Drive

Druncan: A derogatory nickname for the Vancouver Island town of Duncan

Expo: A world's fair held in Vancouver on the occasion of the city's centennial in 1986. It's often said of Expo that "we invited the world and then they didn't leave." Fifty-four governments and industries from six continents participated, and there were over 22 million visitors. It was the biggest event in BC history and helped put Vancouver on the international map. Some of the lasting contributions include Science World, Skytrain, Canada Place Convention and Exhibition Centre, and BC Place Stadium.

The Ferries: A term that refers to the entire BC Ferries Corporation and its fleet, as well as to the often arduous process of travelling by them, e.g., "I was stuck at the Ferries all day and didn't even make it on board."

The Garage: General Motors Place stadium in Vancouver

Garden City: Richmond is officially known as the "Garden City." Victoria, for its part, is known as the "City of Gardens."

God's Waiting Room: A derogatory term for Victoria, reflecting its substantial senior-citizen demographic. The city is also known as "home of the newlywed and the nearly dead."

Grouse Grind: A popular workout and dating activity that involves slogging up a trail on North Vancouver's Grouse Mountain

Hi-yu: A leftover term from Chinook Jargon meaning a massive party

Hollywood North: Although also applied to Toronto, this refers to Vancouver's reputation as a major moviemaking destination

Hongcouver: A controversial nickname for Vancouver, first used by *National Geographic*, which refers to the massive influx of Asian immigrants, particularly people from Hong Kong before and after that city was handed over to the Chinese government

Icky Bicky: The government auto insurance monopoly also known as ICBC

The Interior: Always capitalized, the Interior includes all of British Columbia except the Lower Mainland, the islands and the North Coast. Prince George and beyond is the Northern Interior, typically referred to as "the North"

The Island: Vancouver Island. As opposed to "the islands," which refers to the Gulf Islands

The John: Fort Saint John

Kokanee: It's the beer out here—and also a type of landlocked salmon

Kits: Vancouver's Kitsilano area. Also known as "skits" or "schiz," a reference to the neighbourhood's many homeless people

K-town: Kelowna

The Loops: Kamloops

Lower Mainland: The Greater Vancouver–Fraser Valley district, which is home to the vast majority of British Columbians. It is considered "lower" because most of it is virtually at sea level, whereas the rest of the province is mountainous. Not that anyone refers to the rest of the province as the "Upper Mainland."

Mardi Gras: A term used to describe the period of drug- and booze-fuelled insanity that takes place in Vancouver's Downtown Eastside after residents receive their "Welfare Wednesday" checks at the end of the month

McFamilies: Derived from MCF, the initials of the Ministry of Children and Families

Metrotown: Originally the name of a massive shopping mall in South Burnaby, it is now used to describe the surrounding community

Muckamuck: A Chinook word denoting a chief or someone important, e.g., "That guy from Toronto thinks he's a real high muckamuck."

New West: New Westminster

Nickelfault: A term used to describe a generic style of radio-friendly grunge-lite rock music typified by the popular Vancouver bands Nickelback and Default

No Fun City: A derisive label for Vancouver, applied because of its draconian liquor laws and popularized after it became one of the only major cities in the world to decide against hosting any kind of official Y2K party

Pain and Wastings: The infamous intersection of Main and Hastings in Vancouver's drug-addled Downtown Eastside

Pig's Gorge: An epithet for the city of Prince George inspired by the prevalent sulphide stench from its pulp mill

PoCoMo: The tri-cities of Port Coquitlam (PoCo), Coquitlam and Port Moody

Pogey: Refers specifically to Employment Insurance, not welfare, as it does in the rest of the country

Ridge Meadows: The Maple Ridge and Pitt Meadows region

Rupert: Prince Rupert

Sea to Sky Country: The region stretching from West Vancouver to Pemberton

Skookum: A Chinook word meaning something strong, large or way cool, e.g., "That's a skookum new set of wheels you've got there!"

Splendor Sine Occasu: BC's motto, a Latin phrase meaning "splendour without diminishment"

Slurrey: The oft slurred-against city of Surrey, the car theft capital of Canada. Also sometimes known as Surrey Lanka for its large East Indian population

Squish: The town of Squamish, the self-proclaimed "outdoor recreation capital of Canada." Also referred to as Squeamish or Squampton

Terminal City: Vancouver, an allusion to the city's position as the terminus of the Canadian Pacific Railway

Tweed Curtain: A reference to the "veddy British" affectations of the city of Oak Bay on Vancouver Island

Van: Vancouver. More commonly associated with different parts of the city, e.g., North Van, East Van. Other common nicknames include Vansterdam, Van City and Vangroovy

Vic: Victoria. See above

Vicboria: A complaint against the capital for its reputation of rolling up the sidewalks after dark

TOP 10 REASONS TO LIVE IN BC

10. You don't have to worry if it is going to rain—it's already raining.

9. Everyone else is doing it.

8. Federal politicians almost never visit.

7. The biggest and best university has a nude beach.

6. It has some of the best skiing and avalanche training in the world.

5. The grizzlies and cougars almost never attack.

4. It's fun to recognize local places when you're watching movies supposedly set in the United States.

3. The Canucks are bound to win the Stanley Cup sooner or later.

2. There's lots of cheap sushi and locally made wine.

And finally, the number one reason to live in BC:

1. Shorts and t-shirt weather in the dead of winter.

ABOUT THE AUTHOR

Andrew Fleming

Andrew Fleming is a contributing editor for *Adbusters* magazine and a freelance writer for the *Globe and Mail, Vice, Nerve, Paddler* and many other publications. Since getting his BA in English literature from McGill University, he has also studied film at Vancouver Film School and worked as an actor and stagehand. Andrew currently lives in Vancouver.

ABOUT THE ILLUSTRATOR

Roger Garcia

Roger Garcia immigrated to Canada from El Salvador at the age of seven. Because of the language barrier, he had to find a way to communicate with other kids. That's when he discovered the art of tracing. It wasn't long before he mastered this highly skilled technique, and by age 14, he was drawing weekly cartoons for the *Edmonton Examiner*. He taught himself to paint and sculpt; then in high school and college, Roger skipped class to hide in the art room all day in order to further explore his talent. Currently, Roger's work can be seen in a local weekly newspaper and in places around Edmonton.